Praise for *Pure Charcuterie*

There are plenty of books about charcuterie
but none couple technical know-how with the elo
to language and learning that Leigh employs. Mak   ...cuterie
is indeed an art form. Meredith's artful writing inspires us to be
that kind of artist. Her thoughtful approach to instruction
makes it possible to actually be one. I will refer my own
students to this book again and again for that reason.

CAMAS DAVIS Portland Meat Collective,
Meat Collective Alliance

Meredith Leigh does something with *Pure Charcuterie* that
most chefs strive a lifetime to do—combines the worlds of ethical
meat production with innovative ingredients and techniques such
as koji curing and wild game recipes. *Pure Charcuterie* is a
must-own for amateur and professional butchers alike.

CHEF CLARK BARLOWE Heirloom Restaurant, Charlotte, NC

In this beautifully rendered book, Meredith Leigh takes us
on a poetic journey through the world of charcuterie showing
us step by step the key concepts and principles of home curing for
the novice. I'm excited to embark on the journey she lays out in this
amazing book and I hope to meet you along the way. I guarantee
you it will be a rewarding one, as I don't know of anyone that can
make a description of making mortadella sound poetic, funny,
emotionally engaging and most importantly to the point.

REY TAGLE Instagram: @home_charcuterie

This book will make you hungry. It'll make you dig out the meat grinder someone gave you years ago. It'll make you want to change the world. Meredith Leigh is one of the foremost young authorities on sustainable meat. Her latest book, woven with recipes, philosophy, and poetry, is so much more than a step-by-step on charcuterie. Read it, and you'll see that the ingredients of good food extend far beyond your kitchen.

REBECCA MARTIN Managing Editor, *Mother Earth News*

Pulling no punches, Meredith Leigh balances the scientific "whys" of curing fundamentals, food safety and sanitation, while encouraging curiosity and flavor artistry. Her prose make will you feel like you have a teacher and mentor beside you each step of the way to create salty, fatty, delicious, pure charcuterie.

TANYA CAUTHEN Owner, founder, butcher, Charcutier, Belmont Butchery, Richmond, VA

Pure Charcuterie is the book I've been waiting my whole career for. Meredith takes an approach to creating charcuterie and guiding you through the process that I've never seen before in print. … This is a book for advanced professionals and beginners alike. There has not yet been a book about charcuterie that speaks a more resonate and relatable tone.

JEREMY UMANKSY Larder Master/Owner, Larder Delicatessen & Bakery

In Pure Charcuterie, Meredith Leigh takes the reader on a meaty, and yet artistic journey into the wonderful world of curing meats. This book should be on the pantry shelf of every meat loving maker out there – and even if you don't envision creating charcuterie, Leigh's prose, detail and passionate voice will help you understand the history and process behind the textures and flavors you so savor.

HANK WILL Editorial Director, *Mother Earth News*

Pure
CHARCUTERIE

THE Craft & Poetry OF

CURING MEAT AT HOME

MEREDITH LEIGH

new society
PUBLISHERS

Cover design by Diane McIntosh. Interior design by Setareh Ashrafologhalai
Cover photo by Cindy Kunst / Clicks Photography

Printed in Canada. First printing November 2017.

This book is intended to be educational and informative. It is not intended to serve as a guide. The author and publisher disclaim all responsibility for any liability, loss or risk that may be associated with the application of any of the contents of this book.

Inquiries regarding requests to reprint all or part of *Pure Charcuterie* should be addressed to New Society Publishers at the address below. To order directly from the publishers, please call toll-free (North America) 1-800-567-6772, or order online at www.newsociety.com

Any other inquiries can be directed by mail to:
New Society Publishers
P.O. Box 189, Gabriola Island, BC V0R 1X0, Canada
(250) 247-9737

LIBRARY AND ARCHIVES CANADA CATALOGUING IN PUBLICATION

Leigh, Meredith, 1983-, author
    Pure charcuterie : the craft & poetry of curing meat at home /
Meredith Leigh.

Issued in print and electronic formats.

ISBN 978-0-86571-860-9 (softcover).—ISBN 978-1-55092-653-8 (ebook).—
ISBN 978-1-77142-248-2 (EPUB)

    1. Meat—Preservation—Handbooks, manuals, etc. 2. Cooking (Meat). 3.
Cookbooks. I. Title. II. Title: Craft and poetry of curing meat at home.

TX612.M4L45 2017   641.4'9   C2017-905681-6   C2017-905682-4

Funded by the
Government
of Canada

Financé par le
gouvernement
du Canada

New Society Publishers' mission is to publish books that contribute in fundamental ways to building an ecologically sustainable and just society, and to do so with the least possible impact on the environment, in a manner that models this vision.

This book is dedicated to anyone who does real work every day serving the land, serving other beings, supporting none of society's illusions, and receives no credit, but does that work anyway. I honor you.

And for my loved ones who look me in the eye daily.
You have my heart.

CONTENTS

INTRODUCTION 1

1   **ON INTENTION** 4

Synergy 5

Sourcing 6

Safety / How It Works 9

Equipment and Supplies 13

2   **ON PRECISION** 14

Sausage Primer 14

Sausage Processing 21

Apple Horseradish Sausage 29

Miso & Pickled Ginger Sausage 30

Rabbit Andouille 31

Buttermilk Boudin Blanc 32

3   **ON SUSPENSION** 34

The Terrine 37

Chutney & Confit Terrine 39

Pâté of Thirds 42

Working (Wo)man's Lunchbox Pâté 44

60-20 Suspension 47

Pâté Gratin 48

Mortadella 53

4 **ON WHOLENESS** 56

Dry Curing 59

Wet Muscle Curing 63

Bacon 68

Corned Beef & Beef Pastrami 70

Lardo 74

Tasso Ham 73

Pork Shank Confit 76

Coppa or Capicola 79

Black Pepper Culatello 82

5 **ON COLLABORATION** 84

Fermented Dry Sausages 88

Making a Charcuterie Cabinet 91

Starter Cultures and Beneficial Molds 94

Koji Charcuterie 97

Growing Koji 98

Chile, Mustard & Pickled Celery Salami 104

Calabrese-Style Salami with Vanilla & Lardo 107

Nduja 108

Koji Venison Bresaola 111

Five-Spice Koji Lomo 112

6 **ON CULMINATION** 114

Cooking Sausages 115

Smoking Meat 116

Building Your Own Cold Smoker 118

Serving and Storing Charcuterie 124

Additional Recipes 125

Homemade Horseradish 126

Homemade Miso Sauce 126

Pickled Ginger 127

Fermented Sweet Pepper 127

Pickled Celery Leaves 128

Fennel Pickles 128

Candied Jalapeño Pepper 129

Pimento Cheese Spread 129

RESOURCES 131

ACKNOWLEDGMENTS 132

ABOUT THE AUTHOR 133

A NOTE ABOUT THE PUBLISHER 134

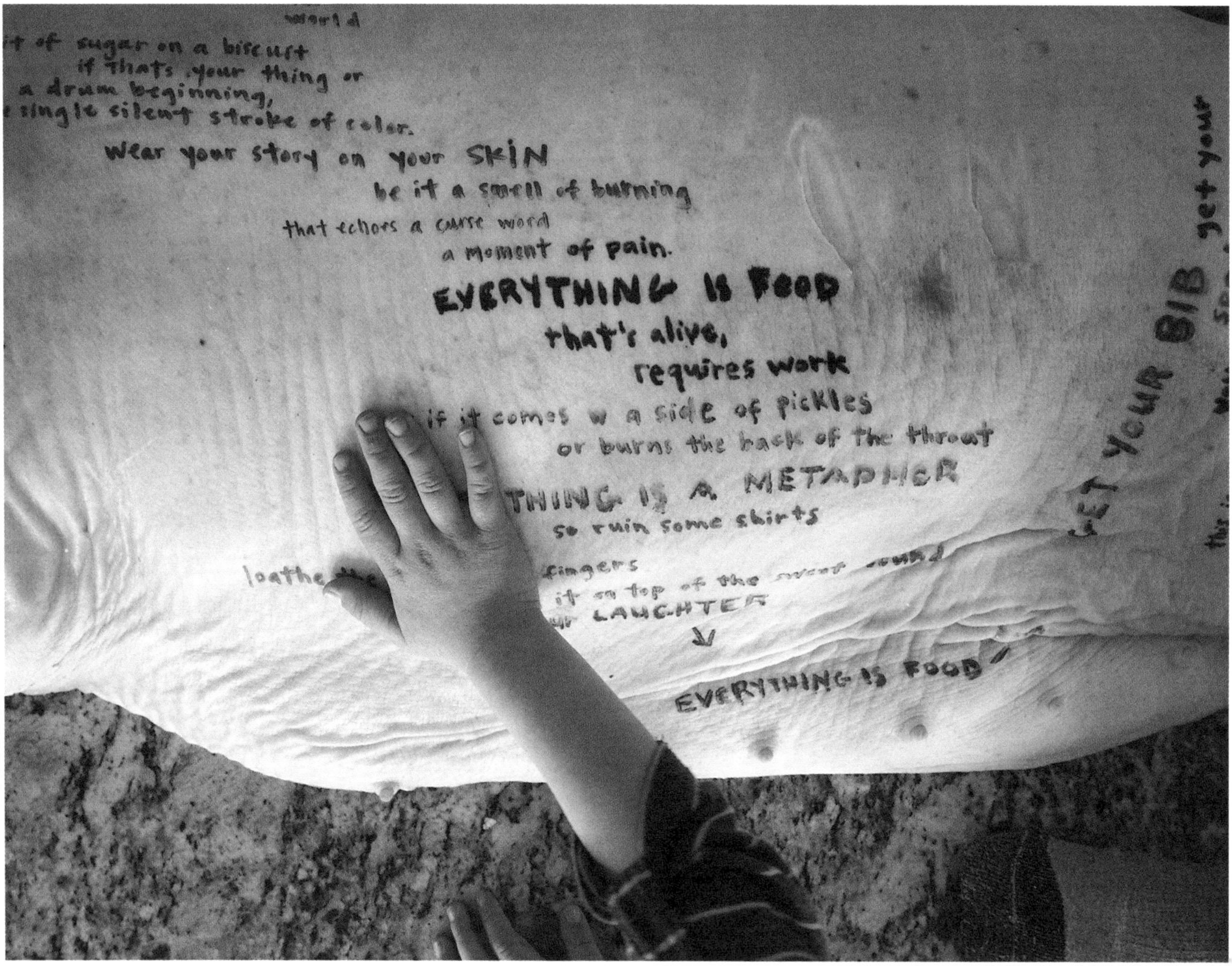

INTRODUCTION

I HAVE WRITTEN ABOUT good food as a sensory journey and a form of activism, one that pleases and awakens the whole being. I believe that food can move us, physically, mentally and even spiritually, provided it is experiential and not severed from its genuine roots. In the world as I know it today, this makes food and media like it more valuable than ever.

As a girl, growing up poor in the city, I was constantly underwhelmed and alarmed with the charade of social performance and the dilution of art in mass entertainment. I was confused. How come the way I felt couldn't be touched in the world around me? Did that mean that it wasn't real? Books, dead writers and poets became a place for me. I dove into a more comfortable subsurface world with art, with writers who must have felt some of the ancient depth and longing that I had felt, with the courage to speak about it, even if only in metaphor. I wanted to create like that, but the academia around literature and poetry was intimidating. I believed there were so many things I needed to know to make art. So I studied, and in studying the art became more lost, in a machine of technique I only sometimes understood. Around that same moment I started growing food, and that became the grandest embodiment of real art that I had ever encountered. It still is.

I gave up writing, then, for a very long time. Instead I lived within organic farming and nature: the soil, the sting of the okra plant, the skins of the fruits and the sticky songs of the bugs. It seemed to me, in this realm, that two and two made ninety. How was such resonant experience, such emotional palpability, possible, just from the raw tools of nature? It was too much. It was everything. As the grandeur of growing food expanded in my life, the fact that it was (and is) so political, so connected and so fundamental added ever more allure. This. This would be my art.

About five years ago, I embraced my writing again. From poetry of loss and beauty to technical tomes on grinding meat, here I am. A writer. Everything is art, suddenly. I can touch what is real through writing. I can touch what is real through farming and food. But now, how can these arts marry into one? How can it then be of service? I write this at a time of deep transition in our culture. A book about curing meat, of all things! How can I convey worthwhile material of this nature to a troubled world? Who can possibly understand the bearing of a cured sausage on a hurried, frightened culture? Would a poem help you understand the importance of seeds? How can I show what is real? Pull your head up from your phone and touch this plant. Cut here. Smell this. Be gentler. Have a taste.

Meat preservation arose from necessity. It is trending now as art. I hope this book can successfully argue that there is no difference between these two things. We need the collusion of art and necessity in our collective mindset, now more than ever. We need to understand that what is real and important is also what is moving and beautiful. It also very often ends up being what is most functional. That is why we are drawn to it. That is why you want to know, and you want to do. To create. That is just it! That you and your people have a history of thrift, rather than the waste you see on a daily basis. That the ones who came before you made trusting marriages with the land, and that you need not only inherit irreverence. That we came from industrious souls, unafraid of mystery and committed to beauty and flavor. In the midst of pop culture and the confusion of our times, you want to see, hear, feel, taste and smell the victory of a genuine craft. You want to become vulnerable to what is softly real, not weakened, and not afraid of what is so distant and out of control. You are, after all, just an imperfect, innocent piece of nature.

I believe that in the search for what is genuine, the answer is to create. Cured meats are works of art that will open you to the land that feeds the animal, the mindful slaughter and butchery of the meat that so affects quality, and the creative possibility within yourself that curates these efforts into flavorful food. Cured meats are growing in popularity, and that is a very good thing. However, the representation of charcuterie as gourmet, over time, has created cultural and culinary blockades against the *best* representation of cured meat, and the accessibility of its creation. In trying to marry art and necessity, this book aims to ensure that we do not engage in the dangerous misconception that the everyday cook will not be able to cure meats. I challenge my students to consider that America is one of the only places on Earth where the rich can steal traditions and even ideas from the poor, *and* convince the poor that they don't want them back.

The cultural attitude du jour is that cured meats are refined, and they are, but not by money or by class as we perceive. While their right preparation is a labor of time, talent and skill, the way we monetize time, talent and skill should receive ample skepticism. Quality cured meats are created by extremely industrious people from meager circumstances the world over. Preserved meat products arose from need and ingenuity, simple resources and pure ingredients. Art, born of necessity. Let us not forget this, and let us also celebrate it, by ensuring that we have twelve-year-olds hanging hams in their closets, and urban homesteaders cold smoking bacon on the stoop.

So therefore, in solemn worship of salt, dedicated to the unfathomable variation in soil, and powerfully dependent on the pig, the duck, the tin-tinged organs, we forge ahead. We want back in there. Let us into the space we can feel all over. We want more of what is real, and we want to savor it, slowly. We want things that are beautiful, meaningful. We want things that last.

ON INTENTION

What good does it do
to lie all day in the sun
loving what is easy?
MARY OLIVER *Starfish* (1986)

THE UNDERPINNINGS OF this book are slightly grandiose. I have been so inspired and so informed by nature and food, that I presume to somehow encapsulate the connectivity of art and sustenance into sausage. At first consideration, this seems ludicrous, even to me. But when the *poof* of spores from a beneficial mold explodes softly in my kitchen, or I can smell in the soil the inkling of a spring supper, I feel like this intention is not ludicrous at all. And not optional.

My simplest of charges in the pages that follow is to situate the reader comfortably in the world of curing meats. Technique and process and principle will rule the day, in that regard. But I refuse to ignore the social, intellectual and spiritual enlightenment that guides that process properly. In other words, there is an attitude and a mindset that I wish to impart, in hopes that it lends to your success, and to a general activism that craft food must address.

SYNERGY

There isn't the space in this book to provide butchery instruction, or thorough discussion of the life, death and processing of the animal as it pertains to the quality and uniqueness of the charcuterie product. That's the stuff of my first book, *The Ethical Meat Handbook*. However, it is the synergy of all these important factors, in addition to the proper knowledge and appropriate creativity of the cook, that make cured meats so delightful.

Taking even a brief moment to consider the incredible interplay of factors that leads to the experience of charcuterie is already mind-blowing. Ponder for a moment, for example, the myriad effects of an animal's life on the composition of its muscle and fat. Here are a few:

- What the animal ate
- How much the animal moved
- How healthy the animal was
- What non-feed inputs were used in raising the animal
- What breed the animal was
- The composition of the animal's parents, and older generations
- The age of the animal at slaughter
- The stress level endured in life
- The quality of the animal's death
- The amount of fat on the body

The list goes on. Add to that some of the factors to consider in processing:

- Whether the carcass was aged
- Whether the carcass was kept at proper temperatures
- Whether the meat was injected with water or other additives
- How well or with what aim the carcass was butchered
- How long the meat or fat has been kept in storage before sale

Again, we could go on. The point of this exercise is to respect the inherent complexity we work with, and to recognize that it is a combination of these factors that lead to the result that is every single animal we eat. It's nearly mind-boggling, isn't it? Just a quick jaunt over the list above sets one's mind afire with the nearly infinite combinations of factors that come into play. This is one of the primary motivations behind the case of Ethical Meat, the subject of my first book. The assertion that Ethical Meat exists, and that it requires input and buy-in from players all across the supply chain, is based on the recognition of synergy.

Synergy is the secret sauce in all systems. It refers to the potential created by many diverse factors combining. It is the fireworks of collaboration. When one thing touches another thing, they create energy and products together that neither single thing can create on its own.

You surely recognize that this is the foundation of cuisine. Pesto is pesto because when basil, garlic, parmesan, olive oil, pine nuts and salt come together, they create a magical goo that wouldn't be possible without all of these components. It would change if you changed any one of them. Its overall impression depends on the distinctness or relative goodness of each of its components, and on and on and on. Dedication to the idea of synergy not only creates a beautiful space in the mind of any cook, but it leverages that space to continue expanding, remaining strong in what we know and can control, and humble in the face of what we don't know and cannot conquer. This combination of kinship with nature and its products and anonymity in the face of creation is the mindset of good learning. Good learning is the chief requirement of sound artistry.

SOURCING

Good charcuterie starts with good meat and good fat. Good meat and fat come from an animal that had a good life, a good death, a good butcher and a good cook. The surest way to find such meat and fat is through direct relationships with farming and farmers.

While many of the recipes in this book are designed around pork, the principles can be adjusted and applied for any species.

Homesteaders working with modest landholdings might consider animals that can be raised there, such as rabbits, ducks or, in some cases, small ruminants. When venturing toward larger animals for beef heart pastrami or confit pork shank, seek out specialty farmers or butcher shops when you can.

The system by which most meat comes our way in America is based on backward economy, poor resource management, coercion of farmers and mechanized suffering, to name a few of its many vices. On top of this, the product lacks flavor and nutrient density relative to meat and fat that can be sourced close to home, from purveyors without allegiance to corporate dominion over the food supply and the soil. That being said, not all local products are superior, and there are some very good people in the world who have no choice but to participate in the ghastly external system. There are very good farmers forced to model their systems as the industry dictates, and not as nature suggests. We, as consumers, or everyday "food citizens" as I like to call us, are indeed the biggest contributors to the backward food industry, and its biggest victims. I say this in an effort to honor the truth, which is simple and whole: Good food comes from good soil and diverse, synergistic systems. I speak this truth with full recognition of reality, which is less simple, and less than ideal: We eat and work within a food system that does not support good food for all. What are you to make of this? Do the best you can, considering the situation.

Look for healthy lean muscle, deep in color and firm but springy in texture. Fat should be creamy and white, and at least somewhat plentiful. This can apply to both intermuscular fat (fat located between muscles and muscle systems) and intramuscular fat (fat within muscles/marbling), however less intramuscular fat could be attributed to breed of animal or feed regimen. Again, the more you can talk to the producer, or the more the butcher can tell you, the more you can select your meat relative to your project, and in good faith toward the ethical meat ethos. As you develop your charcuterie practice, you will be able to recognize quality meat and fat almost instantly, via texture, scent and color.

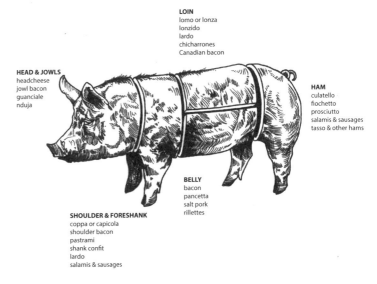

▶ This image depicts the typical American method for pork butchery, and attributes traditional charcuterie preparations to their customary carcass primal.

LOIN
lomo or lonza
lonzido
lardo
chicharrones
Canadian bacon

HEAD & JOWLS
headcheese
jowl bacon
guanciale
nduja

HAM
culatello
fiochetto
prosciutto
salamis & sausages
tasso & other hams

BELLY
bacon
pancetta
salt pork
rillettes

SHOULDER & FORESHANK
coppa or capicola
shoulder bacon
pastrami
shank confit
lardo
salamis & sausages

Most recipes and many traditions dictate a specific cut for each charcuterie preparation. This is many times due to the way a cut lends itself to a process, but it can also be tweaked, based on knowledge of similar muscles within the animal, and based on availability. I am a firm believer in full reverence to tradition, but I also believe good practice and holism require us to evolve tradition to the extent that it best serves the whole. If you are not knowledgeable of butchery, follow the suggestion in the recipe until you gain more experience. As you learn about muscle science and have some sensory experience with butchery practice, you can allow yourself to become more flexible. I have tried to note in each recipe where you cannot afford to be cavalier, and processes or instructions with which you can allow yourself some creativity.

The same can be said for spices, salt and other ingredients. Seek the freshest and most responsible ingredients possible, as these will inform a better product and a better food system. Follow tradition where it serves you, and branch out where you wish to forge new and delicious ground.

For casings, I prefer natural over synthetic. For fresh sausages, I use natural hog casings, for salamis I use natural beef middles, and for larger preparations or whole muscle cures, I use hog bungs and hog bladders. Sheep casings will come in handy if you want to make breakfast links or snack sticks, and beef bungs are used for curing coppa. You will see each of these items pictured with the recipes for which they are used.

The Resources section at the end of the book provides online purveyors for items that you might have trouble purchasing around the corner.

SAFETY / HOW IT WORKS

I am not a germ freak. On the contrary, I grow mold next to my desk on an ongoing basis. Let's be honest — some of our best foods in the world come from our understanding of, and openness to, microorganisms. Chocolate, coffee, tea, yogurt, cheese, alcohol and salami are just a few of the delicious possibilities we've come up with by not being total germ-a-phobes. That being said, we must also have a respect for the harmful microorganisms that can plague our cookery. Charcuterie is a practice in which you can become intimately unafraid of nature, and indeed delighted by its mystery. But you will also need respect for its power. In meat processing, there are a few notable foes of the process. The majority of them, including Campylobacter, listeria, salmonella, *E. coli* and staph can be prevented by cooking fully or preserving thoroughly, ensuring you start with clean product, and maintaining a clean and cold processing regimen. Botulism is in another category, as the deadliest potential pathogen in food preservation. It thrives in oxygen devoid, acidic environments, and can only be inhibited by thorough cooking or use of nitrite (more on that later). Trichina is a parasite of concern in wild game and some pastured animals. Freezing meat for at least 82 hours at less than –10 degrees Fahrenheit (a median temperature for most home freezers) will kill it.

The most important and most basic safety principles are to 1) keep work area, hands, equipment and everything as clean as possible, and 2) keep everything as cold as possible. As meat gets smaller, it needs to be kept colder. This is because the more surface area meat gains (via cutting or grinding), the more breeding ground bacteria is given. You'll notice the particular attention given to temperature as we deal with preparations that include grinding and fine mincing of meat products. In many preparations, you will be encouraged to not only work with frozen meat, but also to freeze parts of your equipment (working parts of your grinder, mixing bowls). You may also want to take a break in the middle of processing, and let the meat chill in the fridge before continuing to ensure everything stays around 40°F, and no warmer. 3) Ensure your projects meet parameters for internal temperature when hot smoking or cooking, and for weight loss when air curing. For the latter, measures of pH and water activity are the most reliable markers of food safety.

An understanding of how charcuterie works, when it works, is essential to preventing safety issues, as well as producing great-tasting products. In addition to common sense sanitary practices and cold storage, we use specific tools to aid our cause. Understanding these tools and their role in the process of meat preservation is essential to grasping the essentials of how charcuterie is even possible.

Salt is a critical player in charcuterie practice. It provides flavor, but it also creates inhospitable environments for many harmful microorganisms. Additionally, salt does the important work of reducing *water activity*, which is a measure of the total water available for microbial activity in the meat. Via the processes of osmosis and diffusion, salt lowers water activity and aids in the dehydration of meat, which is ultimately what preserves it for safe consumption.

Smoke has antimicrobial properties, a low pH and other qualities that inhibit rancidity. In addition, the flavors smoke contributes to cured meats play a major role in charcuterie tradition. (More on smoke in Chapter 6.)

Fermentation reactions give us the ability to alter pH, exclude harmful microbes and welcome friendly ones. (More on the magic of fermentation in Chapter 5.)

Controlled **temperature** and **humidity** (Chapter 5) similarly allow us to tailor the environment to microbes that we want, and discourage those we don't want.

Nitrite prevents toxicity of *Clostridium botulinum,* the bacteria that causes botulism. Most nitrite used in the kitchen is chemically derived, but it is a naturally occurring compound that can be found in the stems of leafy greens, particularly concentrated in the stalks of the celery plant. In addition to inhibiting botulism, nitrites also provide color to cured meat items. While nitrite has caused much controversy in the food world, it cannot be flatly condemned. Research has shown that a person would have to eat more than 14 pounds of cured meat in one sitting to become ill from nitrite poisoning, while a mere half microgram (or less) of botulism can kill them. As we explore methods for curing meat throughout this text, we will also explore situations in which nitrites can be excluded. I encourage skeptics to gain an understanding of nitrite in the environment and in our bodies, and to understand that having control over our own processing by making our own charcuterie allows us to avoid some of the pitfalls of this controversial ingredient.

For example, any time a product will be cooked to temperature (150°F for red meats, and 160°F for poultry) any botulism present in the product will be killed. This means that for warm or hot smoked charcuterie, or sausages poached to temperature, a nitrite is not necessary to ensure safety. People often include sodium nitrite in cooked charcuterie products anyway, because it is a color enhancer. However, when producing cured meats on the home scale, you have the freedom of making your own decision regarding the use of nitrite in cooked applications. Additionally, cooking products that are cured with nitrate produces nitrosamine, a known carcinogen. If you omit the nitrite because you know you will be cooking the product to temperature, you can avoid this concern.

When it comes to fermented meats that are never cooked, nitrates are a requirement for food safety. Whether you obtain the nitrate component from naturally derived celery juice extract or from commercially uniform curing salts, the nitrate and nitrite in these additives interact with microorganisms to render botulism inactive and prevent its toxicity in the product. I find it useful to remind people that these are metabolic interactions, wherein nitrite (which is itself only 4% sodium nitrite and 96% table salt) has been added in small quantities (just 4 oz. per 100 lb. of meat) and has then been changed by microorganisms. Nitrite in cured meats is metabolized into nitric oxide, and the trace amounts of this are then metabolized and used by your own body and the microorganisms your body hosts. To attempt to understand the dynamism of these interactions, and to claim to know their exact scientific effects on our health, is laughable, if you ask me. I say you are part of the nitrogen cycle, as you are of nature. I say absolutism of any form is annoying and egoist. Cure on, friends.

Natural sources of sodium nitrite are available, if you are more comfortable with this approach. The most common source is celery juice powder. It is added to the recipe similarly to a curing salt. Simply follow the instructions of the provider in terms of quantity. Because this is a natural source, there can be inconsistencies in the amount of nitrite contained in a measurable amount of product. Even so, I have used it with success, and know many salumists both commercial and home-based who use it with satisfaction.

Time plays in our favor, both because the ultimate symbiosis with beneficial microorganisms only comes when we allow them the time they need to do their work, and because the slow dehydration of meat is the ultimate determinant of shelf stability.

EQUIPMENT AND SUPPLIES

There are many items you'll want in the kitchen to make your curing projects easier and faster. Remember that people used to do this with stone blades and bladders and rams' horns, so feel free to get as minimalist as you want. Below is a list of equipment to consider. I have listed some of the specific models I use throughout the text.

- Boning knife
- Meat grinder
- Sausage stuffer
- Stand mixer
- Smoker
- Food processor
- Steamer
- Freezer space and refrigerator space
- Various stainless steel pots for poaching and blanching
- Tamis or a fine-mesh sieve
- Various sized mixing bowls
- Digital kitchen scale
- Hooks — bacon hangers and various S-hooks mostly
- Loaf pans or terrine molds

Climate-controlled charcuterie cabinet basically any insulated box wherein you can control temperature and humidity. I have a few refrigerators I have adapted with an external thermometer and a cool mist humidifier. Details for this exact setup can be found in *The Ethical Meat Handbook*.

Casings I use natural casings. These are hog intestines (used for standard size sausage links), beef middles (for fermented salamis), beef bungs (for curing whole muscles), bladders (curing whole muscles) and sheep casings (snack sticks or breakfast sausages). I do use collagen casings and synthetic casings occasionally, mostly for mortadella, hot dogs and bolognas.

- Butcher's twine
- Nonreactive containers for storing spices, soaking casings and holding meats under refrigeration while
- they cure
- Cheesecloth
- Sheet pans/rimmed baking sheets
- Towels and aprons

2

ON PRECISION

How do the oranges divide up sunlight in the orange tree?
PABLO NERUDA *The Book of Questions* (1974)

A FRESH SAUSAGE IS a tremendous thing. Done properly, no one argues, and everyone just grunts. The precise and loving combination of well-raised meat, pure fat and fresh seasonings is one of the kitchen's most open-ended and rewarding vehicles for flavor. Get some snow-white fat, some healthy cold muscle, some whole spice, a few herbs you just tore from the garden, some coarse salt and dry wine and experience real freshness from start to finish. You can create a show-stopping fresh sausage in less than an hour, if you're so inclined.

SAUSAGE PRIMER

My five-year old son was set to have some dental work done, and I was chatting with the dentist about preparing him for the big day.

"Best not to go into detail about what will be happening," the dentist said. "Just… tell him we'll do a bit of work and it will be over in a flash. Kind of like — you don't just go around telling people how sausage is made!"

You can imagine the laugh I choked back at that point. Conversation over, or barely begun. I could go on forever, telling the

▲ Buttermilk Boudin Blanc

dentist just how much time I spend explaining to people how sausage is made.

All that aside, why *don't* we talk more about how sausage is made? In the pursuit of *Pure Charcuterie*, to touch on this story and not get to the root of the matter would be absurd. Why, sausage is not a frightening food item. Dare I say, purer than a casserole? Perhaps the food industry can be blamed for stomach-turning concoctions of otherwise questionable scraps, ground to smithereens and punished with additives that cause us to bristle when we consider their origins. But . . . real sausage?

It is meat, fat and salt, y'all. That's all.

From there, it is a veritable playground for the inventive cook, one of the chief jumping-off places for creativity, and a vessel for profound flavor experiments. It is also the foundation of most charcuterie practice. If you understand and feel comfortable with sausage making, you are more likely to master the finer points of meat preservation.

So we begin with fresh sausage. When we say "fresh" sausage, we communicate very quickly that there is no curing step involved, and no fermentation or drying is expected. This is a mixture of fresh ingredients, intended for cooking relatively soon. It is a supremely easy process, requiring only a bit of knowledge about proper recipe ratios, and a mind opened to delicious possibility.

As with many of the preparations you'll encounter in this book, we turn to a "master" or generic recipe, which informs the ratios of ingredients. If you think about it, all cooking is ratios, so this should not be daunting. Rather, an understanding of ratios is a more proper way to go about mastering any cookery. Understand the proportions of ingredients in relation to one another, respect the precision that ratios provide, and you are suddenly equipped with the ability to edit and create almost indefinitely. Opinions vary on the best master ratio when crafting sausage recipes. I don't scoff or scorn anyone their master ratio. Food is art, and art is subjective. Cooking is making controlled mixtures of ingredients into a beautiful mess. Just like life. My ratio for fresh sausage is below. I encourage you to tweak it as the spirit moves you.

Lean meat	70%
Fat	30%
OF THE ABOVE TOTAL WEIGHT, ADD	
Salt	1.75%
Liquid	10–14%
Spices	No more than 4%, usually much less

Let's explore each component in detail, so you understand the interplay of ingredients, and what to tweak when.

▲ Lean & fat components are weighed separately, to establish the proper ratio.

Lean Meat

When I mention lean meat, I refer to muscle in any animal species (beef, pork, lamb, goat, poultry or game). You want healthy muscle tissue. Avoid meat that looks funny. If it has a lot of blood or hemorrhage on it, don't use it. If it is mushy or gray, dry or damaged, don't use it. Of course, if these imperfections can be trimmed off, that's ideal. Work with what you have to isolate the best-quality lean for your sausage. Cutting corners will produce a product that is either unpalatable or susceptible to rancidity. Trim lean meat to a size that will fit your meat grinder, usually around 2 inches wide and up to 3–4 inches long. You'll want to be sure you've cut out any cartilage, tendons, sinew and opaque fascia (also called silverskin). If you're using an electric grinder, you can worry less about silverskin that you can see through. If, however, you are using a hand-powered grinder, you will want to be especially picky about fascia tissue; de-nude as much as you can, slipping your knife under the silverskin and undercutting it to take it right off the top of the muscle.

If you choose to tweak the lean meat component in your recipe, consider that 70%, as I have outlined here, is about the minimum acceptable ratio. Other master recipes call for 80%, 85% or as much as 90%. Start with these alternatives as you adventure, and you'll more quickly find your sweet spot.

Fat

The most ideal fat for sausage making is firm back fat or superficial (outside the muscles, under the skin) fat from any species. That being said, softer fats from the belly can still be used — they just should not be used exclusively in any recipe. If you have a lot of soft fats or belly fat to deal with, spread it out among several recipes, combining it with quality, firm back fat to ensure a good eating experience. Don't use caul fat (also called leaf fat or cod fat), which is the fat around the organs. This fat has a different melting temperature than other fats in the body, and is best reserved for making pastry lard. Also, glands in the body are usually embedded in fat, so as you trim through, make sure you remove any glands you find. They are beige or olive colored, and easy to spot.

If you choose to tweak the fat component in recipes, remember that it is totally relative to the lean meat component. So whatever your lean meat quantity is, the fat added to it should add up to 100%. If lean meat is 70%, the fat is automatically 30%. If lean is 85%, fat is 15%. You get the idea.

Salt

Quite possibly the most argued ratio among sausage makers. Traditional French *charcutiers* lean toward salt contents of 1.3–1.4%. I have settled on 1.75% for smoked and fresh sausages. I refuse to argue about this point. My ratio is set according to my preference, and when I was the owner of a retail shop, it also produced the most satisfied customers. That being said, as good sausage making provides us infinite metaphors for good living, I say to each his own. If you choose to tweak this component, I urge you to back off rather than add to that 1.75% mark. It is indeed about the highest I would urge you to go in a fresh or smoked product.

The type of salt you use is also crucial to the outcome. I tend toward either sea salt or kosher salt. Be very sure to *weigh* salt, and all other ingredients, rather than measuring it in a spoon. Different types and brands of salt have different weights, so the only way to ensure consistent results is to use that scale.

Liquid

Old-schoolers often just grind with ice, and this is the only liquid component in their sausage, but I find this disappointing to results, and much less fun. Flavor explodes and composition excels when a liquid component is prioritized in fresh sausage. This should not be water but wine, stock, cream, liqueur, fruit juice, kombucha, whatever. I advocate that it is dangerous to prescribe a set percentage on a sausage's liquid content. This should be determined instead by the recipe. If you are composing a sausage with a lot of dry seasoning (which will absorb the liquid) or a particularly astringent ingredient (which will create a dry feeling on the tongue), you will want more liquid in the recipe than for a simpler sausage. Set the liquid component at 10% for recipes with minimal or uncomplicated ingredients, and expect to go up to as high as 14% for recipes that get a little more complex. Any time you create a recipe, there will always be a time to taste test, with the ability to easily adjust before you continue. You can find more info on that in the Sausage Processing section.

Spices

Oh, my spice cabinet. It is a danger to anyone who opens it. If you don't know what a specific seed looks like, or you're not partial to the smell of some random leaf fermenting, beware! I am obsessed with spices and herbs. I'd love to grow, cut, ferment, dry, mix and eat all of them. I trust that as you become enamored with sausage as a way to express your creative whimsy and enjoy fabulous food, you will become a spice freak too. Below is a list of the spices I most often use in sausage making. This is by no means exhaustive.

The ratio for spices is less important than the ratios for lean, fat, salt and liquid. Truly, just add the spices you think will be delicious, and don't be afraid to experiment. I have provided, in my master recipe, a rough "maximum" on dry spices that corresponds with the rest of the ingredients. You may find, however, that you can make a delicious sausage with more than that. Be my guest. My 4% is based on currywurst recipes that are some of the spice-heaviest recipes I know of. That being said, I am a huge proponent of "simpler is better." If you find a reason to put as much as 4% spice in anything but a currywurst, please be in touch, as I would love to hear about that. Otherwise, I'd urge you toward much simpler spice combos, as a rule.

What you put inside of a sausage to season it can vary infinitely, and as you will see in the recipes section we go from simple herbs to miso to pickles to sauces. At the very least, you will want a decent selection of spices in your cabinet, so you can be flexible when you are feeling creative. In addition to whole spice (ground spices lose their flavor quickly, so buy whole and fresh), grow some fresh herbs in pots or in a plot outside the kitchen. Below is a list of spices and herbs that are great for sausage making, and nice to have on hand. Asterisks denote items that are easy to grow yourself and have fresh within reach.

- Allspice
- Anise
- Basil*
- Bay leaf
- Black pepper
- Caraway seed

- Cardamom pods
- Cayenne pepper
- Celery seed powder
- Cinnamon
- Chinese five spice (make your own, see page 112)

- Chive*
- Cilantro*
- Cloves
- Coriander (this is just the seed from the cilantro plant)*
- Cumin
- Curry
- Dill*
- Dried peppers (ancho, arbol, cayenne, habanero, pasilla bajio, guajillo, serrano, and many more)
- Fennel seed
- Garlic
- Lavender*
- Mace
- Marjoram*
- Mustard seed
- Nutmeg
- Oregano*
- Paprika, hot, smoked, and sweet
- Parsley*
- Red pepper flake
- Rosemary*
- Sage*
- Sea salt
- Tarragon*
- Thyme*
- Vanilla
- White peppercorn

SAUSAGE PROCESSING

Preparation

Aside from getting your recipe ratios correct, there are a few other matters to be concerned with when crafting a great sausage. The first is **safety** and sanitation. Please refer to the Safety Section on page 9 (Chapter 1). Prepare your equipment, tools and countertops according to the sanitation recommendations found there.

If you've just flipped over to this page, it is important to remember that ground meat has more surface area, which means a bigger playground for bacteria. To deal with this, we start with clean equipment, clean surfaces and clean hands, and we keep everything just as cold as we can. Colder temperatures slow the activity and reproduction of bacteria.

The second factor is **texture**. How many of us have gazed into a meat case and seen sausages that look like liquid in their casings, or bitten into a sausage that feels like it has barely been ground at

▲ Mix the seasonings into the trim before grinding.

all? Alongside salt and liquid, I believe poor texture is one of the top three reasons a sausage can go wrong. So how do we ensure good texture? In fresh sausage, it is quite simple. Prepare your lean and fat trim meticulously, don't overmix, and plan on a standard grind and half re-grind regimen. (When we get to suspensions and salamis we may get a little pickier.) This means you'll grind the whole mix through, and then take half the mix and send it back through the same grinder plate. Easy.

The third issue is **bind**. This refers to the stickiness of the meat mixture, the good stick-togetherness that makes sausage great. It also refers to how well the seasonings have adhered within the

▲ The parts of the standard meat grinder. Clockwise from left: the body, the
worm, the ring, the knife, and two plates, the fine and the coarse.

sausage mix. How do you achieve good bind? Well, by mixing, essentially. Myosin proteins in muscle cells provide the proverbial glue for
good bind, and you'll pull them out as you mix. Careful not to mix
too much, of course, as we want temperature to stay within the range
that keeps fat intact and texture tuned. If you pull the ground meat
mixture apart and it's sort of stringy, then you're assured a fine bind.
Mix no more. If you leave a ground mixture, seasoned, in the fridge
for 24 hours or more (as when composing a fermented salami, Chapter 5), you'll be blown away by the bind you get. You'll pull that grind
out and it will hold together like bread dough. The best way to ensure
binding of seasonings is by premixing, explained below.

▲ Pre-mixed seasonings and trim in the grinder's food tray

▲ Grinding, and then re-grinding, half of the mixture through the coarse plate

Ensure that your lean meat and fat are well trimmed and cut to size for your meat grinder. You can mix these components together at this point for fresh sausage recipes. I always mix spices and salt (at minimum), and sometimes the liquid component as well, into the trim at this point, and then open-freeze the whole mess on a sheet pan for at least 30 minutes. While you're putting things in the freezer, put the moving parts of your grinder in there, too. You want everything as cold as possible to prevent the melting of fat ("smearing") and the proliferation of any unwanted bacteria.

Some folks like to grind and then season the ground meat, but I contend that pre-mixing results in better bind, safer temperatures throughout processing, and superior distribution of flavor throughout the sausage mix. If you're feeling really awesome, you can leave the trim in its seasonings overnight, chilled (or you can do this after the grinding step to further increase bind). It is not necessary, however, to let the meat rest. Save for open freezing, once you get your ingredients measured out, you are ready to grind.

Grinding

If you are using an electric grinder with any amount of horsepower, work with frozen meat and fat that is pre-mixed with your recipe's seasonings. Grind into a bowl with enough space in it for you to do additional mixing, should you decide to adjust ingredients.

▲ Mixing the two textures together

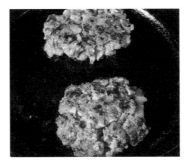

▲ Make up some test patties and cook them to ensure you are happy with the sausage mix and bind.

Put the grinder together according to the manufacturer's directions, and be sure to try to freeze the shaft, worm, knife and plates for a short time before starting. For fresh sausage, I use the coarse plate. I'll push everything through, then send half of the mixture back through the same plate. This produces a variation in the size of the ground product that improves bind and, when mixed together, produces awesome texture for the eater.

Always try to form a small, 2-inch patty of your sausage mix after grinding, and sear it in a cast iron frying pan while your meat mixture chills and you wash your grinder parts. Watch it cook. Does it crumble? Smell it as it warms. Is it burning? Is there enough fat to support good moisture? Listen to it. Is it whining or is it singing? Taste it. Is it too salty? Can you taste all the hopes you had for it, and the synergy between them all? If not, adjust as needed. If so, you're ready to stuff.

Stuffing

Stuffing is optional. Many people sheepishly admit that this did not occur to them easily. If you want to make sausage patties for breakfast, if you don't have time to stuff, if you're out of casing, if you want to incorporate sausage into meatloaf and meatballs; for heaven's sake, don't stuff. If, however, you want a wiener on a bun, or sliced rounds for appetizers, or hanging links for smoking, read on.

▲ Natural hog casings come packed in salt.

▲ Photo of rinsing casings

▲ Loading the hog casings onto the stuffing horn

▲ A vertical stuffer is the best for home use. It is comprised of a canister, a press with an air valve, a housing with a crank handle, a ring and stuffing horns.

See Equipment and Supplies (page 13) for a detailed discussion of casings, and Resources for a list of online providers. If you're spot-reading, just stick to natural casings for fresh sausage. Hog casings will do fine for a standard bratwurst-sized link, and sheep casings will be your go-to for breakfast links. Rinse the casings well of their salt, until they are smooth inside and out. Soak them in tepid water at least 25–30 minutes.

Get your vertical stuffer ready with the mid-sized stuffing horn, and load all the sausage mix into the hopper. You can knead the mix and slap it a bit to get air bubbles out first, if you like. Crank the handle to lower the press onto the mixture in the hopper, which will also evacuate air from the mix via the little air valve built in to the press. Now wet the stuffing horn (or use a little neutral oil on it) and load all the prepared casings onto it, just like bunching up your knee socks or your pantyhose. Don't tie a knot yet. Continue cranking the handle until the meat is just barely coming out of the end of the horn. This will prevent you from stuffing a load of air into the first link. Now tie a double overhand knot into the end of the casing. Keep a small bowl of water, maybe just the bowl the casings were soaking in, nearby in case you need extra moisture along the way. Keep the counter or a sheet pan under the

▲ Crank until just a tad of the meat mixture emerges from the horn before tying off the casing's end.

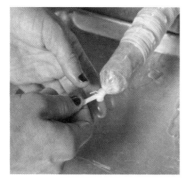

▲ Tie a double overhand knot.

▲ Stuffing requires gentle but capable hands.

▲ Keep the stuffed sausage in a coil as you work.

▲ To link, pinch with your thumb and forefinger where you want the link to occur, and twist.

▲ Twist in alternate directions each time you create a link, to prevent the links from unraveling.

stuffing horn moist, to prevent the stuffed sausage from sticking or tearing.

Crank the handle to start stuffing, keeping your other hand loosely around the end of the stuffing horn to guide the sausage out, receiving it as evenly as possible. You want to stuff it so it fits the casing and isn't saggy or baggy, but you don't want to stuff it so tight that it starts busting when you go to make links. It should feel springy but firm in its casing. As you go, if you find it is stuffed too tight, just pull a little casing off of the horn and massage every-thing out to a better diameter. If you find it is too thin, jam some of the casing back onto the horn so that as you crank, you introduce more sausage into the equation. The point is, you'll have to adjust as you go, especially as you're learning. Eventually you'll whiz right through this process. You may want to keep a sausage pricker or a small sharp knife on hand, to prick out air bubbles as they form, and be sure to position your receiving hand so that the sausage is angled downward slightly as it emerges from the horn. This will prevent additional air from being introduced as you stuff. It also helps to coil the sausage as it emerges, to keep it tidy and allow you to continue receiving easily as you go.

Once you've stuffed all the meat mix in the casings, tie a double knot at the end to seal. To form links, mark off a 6–8-inch section and pinch between your thumb and forefinger to mark the spot where the link will occur. Then, twist at this spot 2–4 times to link off the sausage. Go 6–8 inches down and pinch, then twist 2–4 times in the opposite direction. Continue alternating the direction of your twist as you move up the stuffed sausage. This will prevent the links from unraveling later.

Drying

It is always best to dry stuffed sausages for a bit before you cook them. This enables all the flavors to meld, the casing to form well around each link, and for a thin layer of proteins to develop on the outside of the casing. The protein layer is called a *pellicle*. The pel-licle is especially important if you plan to smoke the sausages, as it will ensure that smoke adheres well to the product. You can hang the linked sausages over dowels to dry them, or simply coil them on a wide plate and keep them uncovered in the fridge overnight. Obviously, hanging ensures even drying around each link, but if it is exceedingly hot in your house or on your stoop, or there are dogs hanging out who might nip at them, or any other such obstacles, you'll have to do what you can.

APPLE HORSERADISH SAUSAGE

I guess a lot of my sausage recipes develop because of leftover things in the fridge. I have become a bit entranced with putting ferments, sauces, pickles and other homemade items into the sausage mix. The horseradish sauce recipe here makes more than you will need for the sausage, so it's a win-win.

Method

1. Mix all ingredients together and open-freeze on a sheet pan. Grind through the coarse plate of your meat grinder, and then re-grind half of the mix. Combine the mix thoroughly and test. Adjust seasonings if necessary before stuffing into the prepared hog casings.

2. This is a versatile sausage, fitting for breakfast or beyond. I think it would fit nicely stuffed into homemade ravioli, accented with fresh fennel and a zingy marinara.

INGREDIENTS

2.5 lb. pork lean trim

1 lb. pork back fat

1 oz. salt

1.5 oz. garlic

1 tart apple, diced

0.2 oz. black pepper

1 cup homemade horse-radish sauce (see page 126)

5 feet of hog casings, rinsed

MISO & PICKLED GINGER SAUSAGE

INGREDIENTS

2.5 lb. pork lean meat

1 lb. pork back fat

1.5 oz. garlic

½ cup pickled ginger,
    minced (to make your
    own, see page 127)

1 oz. salt

0.3 oz. black pepper

¾ cup miso sauce
    (see page 126)

5 feet natural hog
    casings, rinsed

If you are going far enough as to grow your own koji (see page 98), you can make homemade miso for this recipe. I used a light, sweet rice miso for this recipe, but you can use any kind.

Method

1. To make the sausage, mix all ingredients together and open-freeze on a sheet pan. Grind through the coarse plate of your meat grinder, and then re-grind half of the mix. Combine the mix thoroughly and test. Adjust seasonings if necessary before stuffing into the prepared hog casings.

2. Poach to cook and pan sear to finish. When I tested this recipe, we ate the sausage mixed with rice noodles, scant cilantro and loads of butter-seared king oyster mushrooms.

RABBIT ANDOUILLE

Rabbit is on the rise as a nutritious source of lean meat, and it is perfect for the homestead. Rabbit meat has twice the protein of poultry, and a deep flavor that lends well to this Cajun andouille. Dial down the cayenne, and even some of the black pepper, if you don't want too much spice.

Method

1. Mix all ingredients together and open-freeze on a sheet pan. Grind through the coarse plate of your meat grinder, and then re-grind half of the mix. Combine the mix thoroughly and test. Adjust seasonings if necessary before stuffing into the prepared hog casings.
2. Dry overnight, then smoke using pecan wood until the internal temperature of the sausage is 145°F. Serve with peppery rice and some tart tomatoes at the very least.

INGREDIENTS

2.5 lb. rabbit meat

1 lb. pork back fat

1 oz. salt

0.5 oz. black pepper

0.4 oz. dried thyme

0.4 oz. cayenne pepper

2 bay leaves, ground

¾ cup red wine

5 feet natural hog
   casings, rinsed

BUTTERMILK BOUDIN BLANC

INGREDIENTS

1 lb. pork loin meat, lean,
    trimmed for grinding

0.89 lb. roasted chicken,
    or uncooked chicken
    white meat

1.61 lb. pork back fat trim

1 oz. salt

12 oz. chopped onion

1 cup cultured buttermilk

0.2 oz. white pepper

0.2 oz. dried thyme

0.1 oz. ground allspice

0.2 oz. fresh grated nutmeg

0.2 oz. ground ginger

3 eggs, beaten

butter

5 feet natural hog casings,
    rinsed

Boudin blanc, or "white pudding," is a super-traditional sausage, slightly sweet and delicately creamy from the addition of dairy and eggs and a higher amount of fat in the mix. In many old texts, white puddings are regarded as very refined. It's amazing how much less mainstream they are today, especially considering charcuterie's "gourmet" rep. I'd like to bring them back, with a tangy upgrade. Some of the oldest recipes I have found call for adding roasted chicken, rather than fresh, to the sausage mix. That makes this recipe a great use for leftovers.

Here is a perfect example of how we affect texture by messing with ratios. You'll see below that lean and fat are relatively equal in this recipe, and the liquid component has gone up considerably, with the amount of buttermilk and the addition of egg. This will contribute to the smoother texture typical of *boudin blanc.*.

Method

1. Start with frozen meat and fat. If you are using chicken that is already cooked you don't need to freeze it, just freeze the pork loin and back fat. Sauté the onions in some butter until they are glassy. Add to the meat and fat and grind through the coarse plate of the meat grinder. Mix in the spices and then grind everything again through the fine plate of the meat grinder. In a separate bowl, combine the buttermilk and the beaten eggs. Now pour the milk and egg mixture into the meat mixture and put the whole thing in your stand mixer with the paddle attachment. Mix on 2 or 3 until the mixture is quite mousse-like. Taste test. Adjust seasonings if necessary. Stuff into casings and then poach at 170–175°F until the sausages reach 120°F, about 15–20 minutes.

2. It is best to use a strainer or steamer basket that you can immerse in the poaching water, and lift the sausages out when they are finished to prevent them from breaking.

3. When ready to serve, brush the sausages with butter and grill them to sear them off. Serve with mashed potatoes and garlicky greens.

3

ON SUSPENSION

Be joyful, though you have considered all the facts.
WENDELL BERRY *The Mad Farmer Liberation Front* (1973)

I **WAS FEELING DEFIANT** and temperamental recently, so the obvious solution was to make mortadella. The silkiest and most subtly spiced of the meat specialties, mortadella presents a challenge to its creator that requires precision, a light hand, patience and good raw materials. As a result, when I first started my journey into butchery, I avoided it. Now, I regard it as a close but complicated friend.

If sausage is your fun and artsy pal with his shirt endearingly wrinkled, mortadella is a beautiful but volatile girl you never had the guts to ask for a dance. And it is appropriate, I think, for our relationship with food, to see her in each of us. On days when I am my own worst enemy, when my chef mind will not ease up, when I cannot meet even my own standards, and when everything I have created seems to not want to force itself to coexist, I am mortadella. We are flawed beings, striving for optimum presentation. Our lives are an asymmetry of raw materials, plus a little fuss, mostly adding up to exquisite suspension.

Meat suspensions are sausages of sorts, but these preparations, which include bologna, mortadella, pâté, hot dogs and all manner of

▲ From left to right: pate gratin in lard, Working Woman's Lunchbox Pate, and Pate en Croute

terrines, require a bit more graduated knowledge to achieve. Since you understand the ins and outs of grinding meat, creating bind and formulating ratios, suspensions are not far removed from your practice. What separates these preparations from fresh sausages is chiefly the variability in the ratio of lean to fat to liquid, which enables you to nimbly affect texture. Additionally, the suspensions are traditionally served cold, with a few exceptions. Properly, sausages are flavorful mixtures, but the artfulness of the suspension is to develop a relatively heterogeneous situation, wherein meat and seasonings are suspended into a matrix of fat and sometimes liquids.

In many books and resources (including my first) you will hear suspensions referred to as "emulsifications," however erroneous the idea might be that you could actually dissolve meat and fat into one another. A mortadella may feel that way on your tongue, and that is a very beautiful thing indeed, but proper emulsification is not happening with suspensions, as the two insoluble main players are not being forced into one, but rather encouraged into an artful partnership of form and feeling. Once I had shifted this terminology in my head, my visual and visceral understanding of what I was creating changed, and eventually I developed an odd, gentle, and astute respect for the variable and quirky suspension, and its place in the charcuterie.

If you're like I was as a beginner, you might advance into the world of pâtés, terrines and bolognas with hesitation. After all, in America we either think of these preparations as loaves or tubes of the odd and awful bits, and perhaps we were engraved as children with stories about the horrors of their production. Further, as Americans, it is quite possible that some of us have never experienced these products at all, as they have not been popularized in our culture, however many deserving and useful qualities they possess. I would argue that even the upsurge in the demand for charcuterie has not created a deeper understanding of suspensions and their brethren, nor has it raised the bar in the industry enough to encourage their improved production and reintroduction to the public. Therefore, it feels appropriate for me to extol a bit on their virtue.

When I think of pâtés and cold cuts, I think there may be nothing better for the hurried American family seeking nutritious but hearty food for lunchboxes or days out erranding. I think of the health-conscious masses, who are beginning to understand the importance of organ meats in the delivery of minerals and protein to the body. I think of social media photos and magazine spreads that scoff about how beautifully we entertain each other with food. The pâté, the mortadella, the terrine have a home in all of these places. They often include wildly healthful organ meats in such a way that you cannot even discern their specific flavors. They are perfect for a make-ahead meal that you can nip a slice off daily, or for lunches or picnics or appetizers for a crowd. They can be veritable sculptures, so artful in their presentation as to wow even the most seasoned hash taggers or the fussiest of hostesses. Furthermore, I would argue that suspensions are absolutely genius in the thrifty and efficient use of the entire animal. Their rightful incorporation into our understanding of meat eating is essential activism in creating proper economies within the home kitchen (making use of everything you buy), the farm (demand for every product produced) and the animal (respect for the entire, dynamic body).

Now that you are convinced that it would be foolish and lazy for you to brush past the pâté, I will share with you four main approaches to creating a variety of suspensions in the home kitchen. From there, you can launch off into a wonderland of creativity all your own.

THE TERRINE

The word *terrine* is French for earthenware dish. However, the meaning has been expanded to pretty much include all suspensions produced in loaf pans or molds, particularly of whole or chopped food enveloped in aspic. Aspic is a collagen-rich stock; its gelatin content will cause it to solidify when cooled, thereby suspending the whole or chopped food items. The most basic example in the whole animal butcher's arsenal is headcheese, for which a hog's head is brined to tenderize and flavor, then boiled with aromatic vegetables and herbs. The meat and organ matter of the head is cooked, and as it boils it produces its own stock, rich in the collagen proteins derived from the heating of bone, skin and cartilage. To finish the terrine, the meat and organ matter is pulled from the skull, chopped and further seasoned, and then the very stock it produced in cooking is strained and poured over the chopped meat into some kind of form. The entire deal is then weighted and chilled, and eventually turned out onto a platter. In a single pot, one thus creates the most fundamental terrine — chopped meat and other matter suspended in aspic.

Of course, variations on this approach abound. The approach for developing any other terrine is more methodical. One determines the ingredients to be dispersed and suspended in the aspic and prepares each separately, according to the desired end result. One then prepares the aspic. The final step is to patiently layer all elements together and cool before serving.

Below, we explore this process through the preparation of a chutney and pork confit terrine. However, I urge you to grasp how incredibly versatile this concept of suspension is. For an appetizers class, I once created a vegetarian terrine full of edible flowers, suspended in a balsamic-infused stock to which I added a seaweed-derived hydrocolloid called agar-agar that would cause the stock to solidify when cooled. It was beautiful, and not at all specific to meat.

A few specifics to remember when approaching suspensions:

1. They are served cold, which masks or downplays our experience of flavor. Thus, the ratios of salt and seasonings increase compared to fresh sausages.

2. Molding specialties into a form or pan requires some kind of lining in the mold. You may use plastic wrap, strips of fat, bacon or bread. Our recipes below explore all of these approaches.

3. Suspensions require more time to produce. Many will be as easy to mix as a sausage, however, lining the pan and waiting for the item to cook and then thoroughly chill to form will require some planning.

CHUTNEY & CONFIT TERRINE

Feel free to enjoy the fermented fig chutney (page 127) and this pork shank confit (page 76) outside of the mold. All the elements of this dish deserve further exploration on their own merits. The trotter confit, I happen to know, goes very well in homemade handpies. And the chutney, well, just get yourself some cheese and crackers. We have also enjoyed it on pizza, with prosciutto.

Method

1. Roughly chop the celery, carrot and half of the parsley and place them into a soup pot along with the trotter, ear, pork skin, leg cut, and garlic. Cover with the white wine and then cold water until you've got enough liquid to submerge the ball tip or eye of round. Set that on the stove and let it boil, then turn it down to a simmer and let it cook as long as it takes to soften that lean leg cut enough to where it pulls apart. Strain the pot, retaining the stock, and then pull out the lean muscle and transfer it to a baking sheet to cool.

2. Lightly oil a loaf pan and then line it with plastic wrap. Set aside. Scoop out a small spoonful of the stock, place it in a jelly jar and stick it in the refrigerator. Watch it to make sure it sets up into a gel. If it doesn't, you'll need to put your stock back into the pot and put some more bones, skin or feet and ears in it and let them boil down again. You're seeking the collagen in these bits, which will allow your aspic to set properly.

3. When the lean cut is cool enough to handle, pull it apart with your fingers or forks until you have shredded pork. Salt and pepper it to taste, sprinkle it liberally with balsamic vinegar, then chop and add the rest of the parsley. Add any other seasonings you like at this point.

4. Distribute half of the shredded pork at the bottom of the loaf pan, then pour your stock over just to cover the shredded pork. Place the pan in the fridge and wait for the aspic to set. When it has, pull the

INGREDIENTS

Pulled meat from one
   pork shank confit
   (see page 76)
¾ cup fig chutney (see
   page 127)
1 pork trotter
1 pork ear
Some pork skin
1.5–2 lb. lean muscle from
   the pork leg, such as
   the ball tip muscle or
   eye of round
2 ribs celery
2 carrots
1 bunch parsley, divided
   in half
½ corm of garlic, smashed
½ bottle white wine
Balsamic vinegar
Salt and pepper to taste

pan out of the fridge and get ready to add the fig and confit layer. Dot the top of the set aspic with figs from the chutney, as few or as many as you like. Fill the spaces between the figs with confit pieces. Pour stock over this layer to cover, then return the pan to the fridge to set again.

5. When the second layer is set, remove the pan from the fridge and top off the terrine with the remaining pulled pork mixture. Pour stock to cover, which should be all you can fit in your pan. Fold the plastic wrap over the terrine, then cover with foil and place a heavy end-grain cutting board on top of it all, for a weight. Return the loaf pan to the fridge and allow the terrine to chill and set overnight, before turning it out and slicing it into servable pieces. Serve with crackers, pickles and cheeses.

6. Have any leftover terrine, or are you tired of eating it cold? Cut into cubes and freeze. Later, you can place cubes of the terrine inside of homemade ravioli, or into soups.

◀ The first layer
of the terrine

◀ The second
layer of figs and
pork shank confit

◀ The filled terrine,
and aspic being
added before chilling

PÂTÉ OF THIRDS

This is the approach I tend to use for country or rustic pâtés, which tend to include a lean-meat component (usually pork shoulder), in addition to higher quantities of fat and an organ-meat component. Each component is given equal weight in the recipe, roughly a third of the total mixture. In this way, country pâtés, or any pâtés using the rule of thirds, are more like sausages than their relatives, which we explore later.

The pâté of thirds is the most approachable pâté by far, and makes a hearty, no-nonsense cold meatloaf of sorts. The cold presentation of most meat suspensions brings us to an important aspect of their preparation. It is more difficult to discern flavors on your tongue when you are eating cold food than when you are eating food that is warm. Therefore, meat suspensions and products that are served cold generally include a higher ratio of salt to the total weight of lean and fat. They also generally accept more aggressive seasoning.

Additionally, as you get into making pâtés, you will encounter a mixture known as the panada, also referred to as panade. This is usually a combination of cream (though it can be stock or other liquid) and some kind of flour or meal (also breadcrumbs, dry milk powder or grain), and sometimes eggs. Very rudimentary panada will incorporate milk or cream and flour in a 1-to-1 mix, but depending on the other ingredients in the pâté, it will be helpful for you to hold a more flexible space in your mind for these mixtures. Panada is used as a binder for the pâté, but it also lends rich, creamy elements to the recipe that inform flavor and texture in eating.

For the pâté of thirds, the ratio is as follows:

- Lean muscle: 33%
- Organ meat or secondary lean muscle: 33%
- Back fat: 33%

- Salt: 2%
- Spices: 10–15%
- Panada: 10–15%

My dream, at the very least, is for the pâté of thirds to be accepted and loved by Americans for its versatility and its ability to feed us well on the go. I developed the following recipe to encourage this dream along its course. This is meat for the hard-working person.

WORKING (WO)MAN'S
LUNCHBOX PÂTÉ

INGREDIENTS

28.8 oz. pork lean trim

9.6 oz. pork or beef
  liver or heart

9.6 oz. pork back fat,
  trimmed

1.5 oz. kosher salt

1.5 oz. brown sugar

1.2 oz. crème fraîche

0.7 oz. brandy or port

1 egg

2.5 oz. pâté mix*

0.3 oz. orange zest

4 oz. hazelnuts

2 cloves garlic, minced

4 oz. onions, minced

Small handful of parsley,
  minced

Bacon, sliced thin for
  wrapping pâté

*pâté mix
(makes 13 oz.)

3 oz. ground cloves

3 oz. ground coriander

2 oz. dried thyme

1.5 oz. white pepper

1.5 oz. nutmeg

0.75 oz. mace

0.5 oz. bay leaf

This is a thing I make on the weekend, so that during the week I can rush in from the farm, kick off my boots and have a wholly delicious and nutritious sandwich meat in a flash, accompanied by some good cheese, a crusty bread, fresh greens and mustard.

Method

1. Grind 1 lb. of the pork and fat, plus liver, garlic, onion and parsley, through the coarse plate of the meat grinder, then through the fine plate. Set aside. Grind the rest of the pork lean trim and the hazelnuts through the coarse plate and add to the meat and fat mix. Chill. Combine the egg, cream, brandy (or port) and orange zest. Set aside. Measure pâté spice mix and add to panade. Remove meat mix from the refrigerator and place in the bowl of a stand mixer with the paddle attachment. Add the panade salt, brown sugar and spices and mix on speed 2 or 3 for about 2 minutes. Taste test, adjusting seasoning if necessary. Line the loaf pan with plastic wrap, and then with the strips of bacon, leaving a bit of overhang. Fill the pan with the pâté mixture, then fold the bacon over, then the plastic wrap, and then wrap the top with foil. Bake in a water bath at 300°F until the internal temperature of the pâté reaches 145°F.

2. Cool to room temperature, weighted. Then transfer to the fridge and chill completely, overnight, weighted. Turn out on to a wooden board before slicing and serving with crusty bread, cheese and condiments. This pâté will keep in the fridge for at least two weeks. I have not had one last longer than that, so I cannot speak to its further stability.

▲ A typical water bath set-up: the pâtés are wrapped and placed into a larger casserole pan that is filled with enough water to come about halfway up the sides of the pâté pans.

▲ Working (Wo)Man's Lunchbox Pâté components

▲ Working (Wo)Man's Lunchbox Pâté, assembled

▲ Working (Wo)Man's Lunchbox Pâté, finished

▲ Working (Wo)Man's Lunchbox Pâté

▶ Grinding pâté through the fine plate of the meat grinder. This process can be repeated to create finer texture.

60–20 SUSPENSION

The 60–20 suspension seems to be the popular way to feature organ meats. I use it religiously in producing mousses and liver pâtés, and it has not failed me yet. The differentiation is rather simple. You are composing a suspension of two main players — an organ meat and fat. Virtually all other instructions and considerations for the pâté of thirds also hold true here, though the panada may be more prominent in the recipe, as the binding action of myosin (which comes from muscle) will be absent when working merely with organs and fat.

To more finely reduce the texture of any pâté, use a combination of the coarse and fine plates of your meat grinder, or just run the mix through the fine plate several times. The more grinding and mixing you do, recall that you may need to stop and chill the mix, so that it does not rise too much above 39°F. Additionally, there will be times when you may want to sieve the mixture, or force it through a tamis or chinois, to screen out larger bits and create a pâté that is supremely silky. If this is the case, you will simply dump the entire mixture, after grinding, into a fine mesh sieve, or a tamis or chinois for even more discerning results, and press it through (this takes patience and time!) into another bowl.

The ratio for a 60–20 suspension is as follows:

▲ Sieving the mixture to isolate the finest texture, if desired

- Organ meat: 60%
- Back fat: 20%
- Salt: 2%
- Spices: 10–15%
- Panada: 10–15%

I use the 60–20 suspension in combination with some of your terrine-making skills to produce pâté gratin here. Gratin refers to the inclusion of some pre-cooked ingredients, in this case fermented peppers and sautéed mushrooms. We will achieve two pâtés, to help you master different principles; for one, the pan is lined with back fat; for the other, you will envelop the pâté in a pastry to create a beautiful pâté en croûte. The filling for both is the same.

▲ Comparison of 60–20 pâté mixture that has been passed through a tamis (above) and a pâté mixture that has not (below)

PÂTÉ GRATIN

INGREDIENTS

Filling for both molds

2.4 lb./38.4 oz. duck or
  chicken liver
12.8 oz. pork fat
0.8 oz. kosher salt
0.1 oz. ground rosemary
0.3 oz. black pepper
0.6 oz. cane sugar
0.6 oz. quatre épices
2.7 oz. sautéed assorted
  mushrooms, the wilder
  the better
2.7 oz. fermented sweet
  pepper (see page 127)
1 egg
2 Tbsp dark rum
1 Tbsp fine ground cornmeal
Splash of cold heavy cream

Pâté dough for
pâté en croûte

8 oz. all-purpose flour
0.75 oz. non-fat dry milk
⅛ oz. baking powder
¼ oz. kosher salt
3 oz. unsalted butter
1 egg
½ Tbsp apple cider vinegar
2–3 oz. whole milk

Equipment needed: meat grinder, mixer with paddle attachment, 2-cup terrine mold for pâté en croûte, 2-cup loaf pan for pâté in lard, plastic wrap

1. Combine the flour, dry milk, baking powder and salt in the bowl of a food processor. Add the butter, cut into pieces, and process until crumbly. Add the egg and cider vinegar and transfer to a stand mixer. Mix on low to medium speed, then add the whole milk until the dough forms. It should be dry (not sticky) but hold together well. Wrap the dough and refrigerate it until you are ready to assemble the pâté en croûte.

FOR PÂTÉ IN LARD

1. Obtain a strip of back fat, about 10 inches long, frozen and then sliced into paper-thin 2-inch strips.

ASSEMBLY OF PÂTÉS

1. You can grind the filling ingredients all together for both molds. To do so, first place the moving parts of your meat grinder and the bowl you plan to use into the freezer. Then mix up the panada so it can be chilling in the fridge while you grind. In a small bowl, stir together the rum, egg, cornmeal and cream. Set aside in the refrigerator. Next, assemble the grinder, and combine the duck or poultry liver and the pork back fat with the rosemary, salt, sugar and quatre épices, and pass it all through the fine plate of the meat grinder. Run it through a second time if you so desire. Stir the cold panada into the cold meat mixture, and allow everything to chill in the fridge while you sauté the mushrooms and wash the grinder parts.

2. *To assemble the pâté in lard*, line a loaf pan with the thin strips of back fat, as thoroughly as you can. You may want to first line the loaf pan with plastic wrap to make the outside of the pâté more uniform.

▲ Line the loaf pan with the strips of back fat.

▲ Fill the lined mold ⅓ full with the meat mixture.

▲ The second layer is the mushrooms and fermented pepper.

This is completely optional. Make sure the strips of fat overhang the loaf pan enough to allow you to fold them over the pâté once it is filled.

3. Fill the lined loaf pan ⅓ of the way with the meat and panada mixture. Then add a layer of mushrooms and fermented peppers, until the pan is ⅔ full. Fill it the rest of the way with the meat and panada mixture. As neatly as you can, fold the fat strips around the top of the pâté until all the ends are tucked in. Cover with foil and bake in a water bath at an oven temperature of 300°F until the internal temperature of the pâté is 155–160°F. Remove from oven and place an even weight over the pâté, until it cools to room temperature. Then transfer it to the fridge, weighted, to chill overnight before turning it out and serving.

▲ Fill the remaining space with more meat mixture. It will shrink as it cooks, so fill it quite full.

To assemble the pâté en croûte, remove the pastry dough from the refrigerator, unwrap it, and roll it out to ¼-inch thickness, on a floured board. Cut the rounded edges to produce a large rectangle. Grease the terrine mold with a neutral oil, then line the pan with the dough, carefully, leaving overhang to fold over the top of the pâté filling.

Fill as described above — first with meat mixture, then mushrooms and fermented peppers, then more meat mixture. You may decide to pipe in the meat mixture to get ultimate uniformity in distribution. If you do not have a pastry bag and tip, you can force the

▲ Arrange the ends of the strips of fat so that you create a neat package.

▲ Roll out the pastry and trim the rounded edges to form a large rectangle.

▲ Fit the dough into the mold, carefully, ensuring there is overhang.

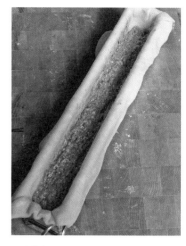

▲ Fill the lined mold ⅓ full with the meat mixture.

▲ Add the second layer of fermented peppers and mushrooms.

▲ Fill the remaining space in the mold with meat mixture.

▲ Trim the pastry as needed, and fold it over the pâté.

▲ Cut a vent in the pâté using a sharp paring knife.

▲ Fashion a chimney using aluminum foil and insert it into the vent.

▲ The finished pâté en croûte

meat mixture into a ziplock bag and cut the corner off. Squeeze from the top to pipe the mixture into the mold.

Trim the dough using a sharp paring knife, and fold it neatly over the pâté, tucking in the raw edges. Using a small knife, cut a vent somewhere into the pâté. Fashion a chimney to fit into your vent. This allows steam to escape without the hole shrinking as the dough bakes. Brush the top of the pâté with a mixture of 1 egg and a little bit of milk. Bake the pâté at 450°F for 15–20 minutes, then reduce the oven to 350°F until the pâté reaches an internal temperature of 160°F.

MORTADELLA

Hopefully I have said enough to make you want her, but this is the grand preparation, which will fill you with a sense of achievement. Mortadella is very much like bologna, however true bologna does not include whole spice. If you'd rather have bologna, feel absolutely free to omit the whole spice in this recipe, and you will not be disappointed. That being said, bologna has many variations, so you can alter the grind process for coarser textures, and tweak the spice mix, and still have bologna.

Producing the finest textured suspension, as in the case of mortadella, usually involves what is known as the 5–4–3 ratio of sausage making. That is, by weight, 5 parts lean meat, 4 parts fat, and 3 parts liquid. This ratio will come into play in the following recipe, as well as higher ratios of salt and spice; other than that you are making a very large sausage. You will notice that I have included ice as the entire liquid component. This is because I wanted a traditional recipe, but also because mortadella must remain very cold in its processing to preserve its texture. By all means, take some stock and freeze it, and have that as your liquid component, if you dare.

One ingredient that may stand out to you is the dry milk powder. It is included as a binder here, and should not be taken lightly.

Lastly, you will notice the inclusion of curing salt #1, or pink salt. Many people include a curing salt to their mortadella, but this is chiefly for rosy coloration; you may absolutely omit it. (More about why and when you might want to do this can be found in Chapter 1).

INGREDIENTS

Mortadella

2.1 lb. / 33.6 oz. lean
    pork trim
1.65 lb. / 26.4 oz. pork
    back fat
2½ cups / 20 oz. crushed ice
1.6 oz. salt
0.8 oz. pure cane sugar
0.5 oz. fresh ground nutmeg
0.24 oz. cinnamon
0.24 oz. cayenne
0.24 oz. coriander
0.2 oz. curing salt #1
1.92 oz. dry milk powder
0.5 oz. garlic
4 oz. back fat, cut into ½-inch
    or 1-inch cubes (omit if
    you want a more proper
    bologna)
1.36 oz. whole black pepper-
    corns (omit if you want a
    more proper bologna)
4–5-inch diameter x 20-inch
    long collagen or plastic
    casing, rinsed

Method

1. Place the moving parts of your meat grinder and the bowl you plan to use into the freezer. Meanwhile, blanch the 4 oz. of cubed back fat for 10–12 seconds, then set aside. Soak your casing in room temperature water until you are ready to stuff.

2. Assemble the grinder, and send all ingredients except for the

peppercorns and the blanched back fat through the coarse plate of the meat grinder. Repeat. Chill the mixture while you exchange the coarse plate for the fine plate on your grinder, then send the mixture through this plate twice as well. Chill the mix while you wash your grinder parts.

3. In a stand mixer with the paddle attachment, combine the meat mixture, blanched back fat and peppercorns, and process on low to medium speed until well combined, and the mixture is quite leggy. Chill while you assemble your stuffer and prepare a large kettle of water, with a few generous pinches of sea salt. Place the kettle on the stove top and begin bringing it to a temperature of around 170°F.

4. Place the mortadella mixture into the stuffer's hopper. Using the largest stuffing horn available with your stuffer, pull the casing as far onto the horn as possible, and begin cranking the meat mixture into it, keeping an even and tight fill as you progress. When you've stuffed everything in, tie off the end with butcher's twine, and carefully lower the mortadella into the poaching water. Monitor the temp as it cooks (it will take 45 minutes to over an hour, at least) to ensure the water stays just under a boil. Try not to temp the mortadella until you are pretty sure it is done, unless you have an infrared thermometer. The hole created by a traditional meat thermometer can allow water into the casing, which can screw up your texture quite a bit.

5. The temperature of the mortadella should be 145°F internally. When it is ready, remove it from the poaching kettle and plunge it into an ice bath or a tub of the coldest water you can muster. Allow it to chill there, then place it in the refrigerator to chill completely.

6. To serve, peel back the casing and slice as thin as you can manage.

ON WHOLENESS

... Some things
you know all your life. They are so simple and true
they must be said without elegance, meter and rhyme,
they must be laid on the table beside the salt shaker,
the glass of water, the absence of light gathering
in the shadows of picture frames, they must be
naked and alone, they must stand for themselves...
Can you taste what I'm saying? It is onions or potatoes, a pinch
of simple salt, the wealth of melting butter, it is obvious
it stays in the back of your throat like truth
you never uttered because the time was always wrong,
it stays there the rest of your life, unspoken,
made of that dirt we call earth, the metal we call salt,
in a form we have no words for, and you live on it.

PHILLIP LEVINE *The Simple Truth* (1994)

EVER SINCE THE natural world has brought me to my deepest node of vitality, I have pondered and puzzled about our human tendency to deconstruct everything. I have it. I've been acutely analytical since I was a child, and wildly subversive. As soon as I started to pay attention to the world, and see human constructs for what they are, I followed every urge to strategically

unravel things, to ask whether they were real or useful, and then, if I felt inclined, to reimagine them into something somehow better. This tendency serves me well most days, but sometimes it becomes an undoing that is more complicated than thrilling, and more unnecessary than it is meaningful. The world is rife with things I'd like to take apart and redesign these days, in service of morality, soulfulness, integrity and joy. I'm working on a balance, of seeing when total revolution of thought and practice is warranted, and where it is perfect, gentle and totally appropriate to just leave things whole and unburdened.

After all, my main lamentation of agriculture, and dietary hullabaloo, and culinary culture, is that we are missing a holistic perspective that will drive resilience, flavor, community and economy. Our scientific approach of disassembling and reassembling has left us short on information about synergy and interaction, a main artery in our understanding of reality and proper participation, especially with the natural world.

Whole-muscle charcuterie is your countertop metaphor for this crusade toward a finer incorporation of wholeness. It's about letting the muscle, or group of muscles, be what they are: a consortium of tissue and action and fat stores, taken and preserved, and that is just that. In this chapter we explore several methods for preserving whole muscles, and introduce the concept of salt curing, a stage in the process not yet encountered in your fresh sausage and suspension adventures.

Recall from Chapter 1 that what cures meat ultimately is a slow process of dehydration. The chief contributors to this dehydration are salt and time. Through the process of osmosis, salt pulls water out of the muscle, thereby lowering the *water activity* of the meat. Water activity is a measure of the water in the meat that is *available to bacteria*. Essentially, this means we are measuring the water available for biological reactions, which have a giant bearing on food safety. This is different from the total water in the meat. Take, for example, a raw piece of meat that is frozen. Before freezing, it is considered to have a very high water activity. As the meat freezes, it reaches a water activity of 0, because all the water in the meat has turned into ice crystals, and is unavailable to microorganisms. There is still water present, but the water activity is 0 because the water is not an actionable medium for bacteria. Take the meat out of the freezer, and as it thaws, its water activity, measured in units Aw, begins to rise.

For those wanting to understand this more, it is helpful to know that Aw is a ratio measurement. It compares the vapor pressure in the food to the vapor pressure of regular water. This ratio tells a story about how likely water is to move from the food product into the cells of any microorganisms that are present (also an osmotic reaction). Since microorganisms cannot do their work without a certain amount of water, when we achieve a specific level of water activity, the food is considered to be shelf stable. As a basis of comparison, raw meat generally has Aw near 1. Salami has Aw of 0.82 or less.

Salt curing refers to a step in the curing process wherein salt is used to lower water activity, and is also often combined with other spices to diffuse flavor throughout the meat. There are two broad methods for salt curing meat products: *dry curing* and *wet curing*. They can also be combined.

DRY CURING

Dry curing is the curing process used for most non-cooked charcuterie items, like prosciutto, guanciale, lomo, and more. It involves mixing salt, usually a few spices, often garlic, and sometimes sweetener, and evenly distributing them over the surface of the meat. The meat is left to cure about a day and a half per pound, then rinsed and dried before moving on to the next stage of the process. What is that next stage? Well, it depends on the preparation. After salt curing, many whole muscle cuts go on to be smoked (think bacon) or fermented and dried (think prosciutto).

In whole muscle curing, you'll be centrally concerned with the ratio of salt to the weight of meat, and that will be the defining factor in your recipe. You'll also be including a curing salt, whose quantity you'll fix based on the weight of the meat. All other additions, such as garlic, sweetener, black pepper, cinnamon, or beer for that matter, are determined entirely by the salt and the meat.

In dry curing, salt ranges from 2.5–4% of the weight of the meat product. For products that will eventually be cooked, such as bacon or some hams, settle on a point within this range that suits your taste best. For products that will be fermented and dried such as lomo or prosciutto, figures in the 2.5–3.5% range will be best, so as not to overwhelm the palate, while still providing enough salinity to exclude a host of harmful microbes. As far as ratios are concerned,

▲ Evenly spread the cure mixture over the surface of the meat.

▲ Press the dry cure into the meat's surface with your hands.

▲ Sirloin with tasso ham dry cure

that is all you need — the weight of the meat, from which you can calculate the amount of salt. Add other seasonings as your creative urges lean. Master recipes are listed below to get you started. You'll notice that there is an optional sweetener included at exactly half the volume as salt. This is a standard ratio for dry cures that include sweetener in their mix. Remember that sweetener is widely variable. Some recipes require none at all, while sugar-cured hams and other traditional preparations call for as much as twice as much sugar as salt. For recipes where I have included it without noting that it is optional, I am recommending it as a flavoring agent, and including it will get you the familiar flavor you are used to. Feel free to omit it entirely, but when you get to salami recipes in the next chapter, you'll need to be more careful. Often, in fermented foods, sugar is included as food for the microorganisms, and tampering with it in the recipes will lead to less than optimum results.

Sodium nitrite (Cure #1) recommended quantities for dry cures are 4 oz. to 100 lb. of meat, or 0.2 oz. for 5 lb. of meat. For whole muscle cures, you can legally use 4 times this much, but I have cured whole muscle safely for years using the minimum recommendation, which is for ground product.

Sodium nitrate (Cure #2) recommended quantities for dry cures are 3.5 oz. to 100 lb. of meat, or 0.175 oz. per 5 lb. of meat. You can also legally use up to 4 times of Cure #2 for whole muscle preparations.

To prepare a dry cure, weigh all ingredients carefully, then mix thoroughly. Pass the dry cure through a sieve to remove any clumps. Clumps can cause "cure burn," or points in the meat where a higher concentration of salt produces a more drastic drying effect, which can lead to off flavors, poor texture, and discoloration. Rinse the meat and pat it dry, then lay it on a sheet pan or in another nonreactive container. Carefully tip the container of dry cure to evenly sprinkle the mixture over the surface of the meat, roughly the thickness of a dime. Press the dry cure into the meat's surface with your hands.

▲ These pork belly cuts have salt cured for 9 days, and are ready for smoking.

Flip the meat over and repeat on the other side, flipping and repeating until you run out of cure mixture. You can also distribute half of the cure over the meat's surface, and then save the remaining cure to apply later. I call this a "split cure," and it is traditional in many preparations.

Once you've applied the cure, you'll want to label the product with the date, weight, and any other information you'll want to remember (percent salt content is common). Refrigerate the curing meat for a day and a half per pound, overhauling it (turning it

INGREDIENTS

Master Dry Cure Recipe

Per 5 lb. of meat:

2.8 oz. salt

1.4 oz. sweetener (optional)

0.2 oz. Cure #1

**Wet Cure for Beef,
Lamb, Goat, and Pork**

Per gallon of water:

2 lb. kosher salt

Up to 1 lb. sweetener
    (optional)

Spices (optional)

4.2 oz. Cure #1

**Wet Cure for
Poultry or Fish**

Per gallon of water:

½ lb. kosher salt

¼ lb. sweetener (optional)

Spices (optional)

4.2 oz. Cure #1

over every day, or at even intervals) to ensure that it cures evenly. If you are planning on a split cure, remove the product after half of the allotted time and administer the remaining cure mixture over its surface, then return it to the refrigerator for the remaining time allotted.

When the meat is finished salt curing, you'll encounter a noticeable difference in its texture and color, finding it much firmer and darker in color. This is a sign of success! Remove it from its container and rinse it thoroughly, then pat it dry and let it rest and dry while you prepare the next phase in the process. Remember that the next step will be determined by your recipe or end goal. At this point, you may go on to smoke the meat, bake it, or hang it to ferment and dehydrate. Remember that after the salt curing step, the meat is not yet finished or shelf stable. I find this is a common misconception in America. Because we have no umbrella term for preserved meats like *charcuterie* or *salumi,* we tend to refer to groups of preserved meats as *cured meat.* This has led more than one beginner to assume that a "salt cure" is all there is to it, when truly, the curing step is only the beginning of the process of meat preservation.

It is best practice to weigh the meat again after it is finished salt curing. Record this weight in the same way you recorded its beginning weight. Tracking weight loss throughout the process is a good way to keep track of the progress of the meat's eventual dehydration, and thus its successful preservation.

WET CURING

Wet curing is similar to dry curing in its ultimate action on the meat, but it simply diffuses the salt, sweetener, and spice mixture into water or other liquid. Many people refer to this process as "brining" the meat, so you may hear it referred to this way. However, be aware that there is brining used strictly to tenderize and flavor meat and brining used to salt-cure meat. Curing brines and flavoring brines differ drastically in their salt content, so in general I strive to refer to curing brines as "wet cures" and flavoring brines as just "brines." You will most often find both words used in curing applications.

Wet cures can be mixed up in a bucket and the meat submerged into them, or they can be pumped into the meat using meat syringes. It is also possible to pump a wet cure into a muscle, and rub it on the outside with a dry cure. I call this a "combo cure" — a combination of wet and dry curing techniques.

Wet curing uses many different ratios of salt to liquid medium, based on the type of meat being cured and the desired cure time. This is the best thing about wet curing: the saltier the brine, the faster the cure. This saved my skin a few times when I owned my own shop. Oops! Easter is around the corner and we forgot to brine the hams! No worries, jack up the salt in those wet cures and get the hams ready in no time. Salt in any liquid solution is measured in degrees of salinity, using a tool called a salometer. Professionals who use these tools can tweak salt in many ways depending on how they want the cure to perform. Luckily for you, different degrees of wet cure have been pre-recorded and widely shared, so you only need to search "brine tables" or "brining tables" online to find a host of different approaches to creating wet cures. The simplest forms of these tables will tell you, per gallon of water, how much salt and how much nitrite to add to create a specific degree wet cure. I tend toward 70-degree wet cures for most red meats and pork and 20-degree wet cures for poultry and fish. Note that the "water" can also be stock, beer, or other liquid.

◀ A trimmed beef heart,
with wet cure ready

▲ Beef heart in wet cure

Nitrite quantities for wet cures are based on the amount of salt you are adding to the cure, as well as regulations on parts per million for food safety parameters. The "pick-up" — #1 the amount of the wet cure the meat actually absorbs — can also vary based on the technique used to expose it to the cure. In the industry, meat is injected with needles, pumped, tumbled, or simply immersed. Each of these techniques can alter pick-up. For this reason, I won't go into much detail about pick-up and nitrite conversion. The vast majority of homesteaders are immersion curing (submerging meat in a bucket of brine) or, less frequently, pumping, and in both of those cases we can assume a 10% pick-up of the cure, for which the recommended nitrite quantities are listed below.

Method

1. To prepare a wet cure, gently heat the smallest amount of water you need in order to dissolve the salt and any sweetener you've included in the recipe. Meanwhile, pour the remaining liquid into the bucket or bin that you'll use for the meat, and add the curing salts plus any spices or other ingredients. Set the bucket aside. When the salt and sweetener are dissolved in the heated water, remove the pot from the heat and allow it to cool completely to room temperature. You may add ice to speed the process, but note that this will dilute the cure, so you must factor that in. When the water is cooled completely, pour it into the bucket with the remaining ingredients, then transfer the bucket to the refrigerator. You want the wet cure to be completely chilled before you introduce the meat to it. Placing raw meat in warm liquid alters the proteins on the outside of the meat surface, in a sense par-cooking or poaching the outside of the cut, which is not what you want.

2. Once the wet cure is chilled completely, you can add the meat. Weigh it down with a plate or other object to keep it entirely submerged in the wet cure. Every day, or at regular intervals, remove the weight and turn the meat to ensure it is evenly curing. If you are using the recipes from above, you'll keep the meat in cure one to one and a half days per pound before removing it, rinsing, and drying. Weight the meat once again, recording its weight after wet curing, and then proceed to the next step in the recipe or process, which could be smoking or fermenting and drying.

BACON

INGREDIENTS

Per 5 lb. piece of pork
belly, skin on:

2.8 oz. salt

1.4 oz. brown sugar

0.7 oz. fresh ground
black pepper

0.2 oz. Cure #1 (optional,
because you will
cook the bacon
before eating it)

Bacon can be made with any part of the hog, but in America we tend toward the belly. Canadian bacon is made from the loin cut, and many folks are partial to shoulder bacon, produced from the collar. Leave the skin on during the cure and while smoking. This achieves two things: ensures the bacon isn't too salty and makes sure the skin will keep moisture in the meat while it cooks.

What differentiates bacon from pancetta is that it is cooked. You can bake it in the oven and it will still be bacon. Traditionally, however, bacon is salt cured and then smoked. For best results, cold smoke it. (More info on smoking in Chapter 6.)

You will need to use a nitrite, in the form of Cure #1, ONLY if you do not plan to cook the bacon to temperature at any point during the process. This is because cooking a product to temperature kills botulism bacteria, so if you hot smoke the bacon, or even if you plan to slice it and fry it as is traditional in America, you can omit the nitrate all together. If you plan to cold smoke the bacon, or if there are any applications for that cold-smoked product that do not call for cooking the bacon, you must use Cure #1 to ensure the product's safety.

Method

1. Mix the cure ingredients evenly, and sieve if necessary. Distribute over the belly evenly, and place in a nonreactive container, labeled clearly with the weight of the cut and the date. Cure a 5-lb. cut in the refrigerator for 7–8 days, then remove it, rinse, and weigh again. Allow the meat to dry as you prepare the smoker. You can even set a box fan in front of it to get it extra dry. The drier a piece of meat is, the more readily smoke will adhere to it. If hot smoking, smoke the bacon at temperatures no higher than 200°F, until the internal temperature of the meat is 140°F. Cool to room temperature, then store in the fridge until ready to serve. To serve, peel back the skin, slice off strips, and fry on medium heat until perfectly crispy.

2. If you are cold smoking the bacon, smoke it at temperatures no higher than 80°F until it has lost at least ⅓ of its weight (that's the weight you recorded *after* salt curing the belly). If you plan to cold smoke the bacon and you do not plan to fry it before serving, you must use Cure #1 during the salt curing step to prevent botulism. See Chapter 1 for more information on the role of nitrates.

CORNED BEEF &
BEEF PASTRAMI

<hr>

INGREDIENTS

Corning Brine

2.5 qt. distilled water

5 Tbsp kosher salt

5 Tbsp evaporated cane
   juice crystals

2 Tbsp Cure #1 (optional)

1 Tbsp black pepper

1 Tbsp allspice

½ tsp garlic

¾ tsp red pepper flakes

1 tsp bay leaf, crushed

5 lb. beef brisket or 5 lb.
   of beef heart (it will
   take a couple)

Pastrami Rub

2 Tbsp black pepper

2 Tbsp coriander seeds

2 cloves garlic, minced

1 Tbsp mustard seed

1 Tbsp sweet paprika

1 Tbsp cinnamon

Few people realize that corned beef and pastrami are so closely related. Corned beef is wet cured and boiled until cooked, and pastrami is wet cured via the same process, parboiled, and then rubbed with additional seasonings and smoked. This recipe gives you the approach for both, so you can go either way.

This recipe uses beef heart, because using the whole animal is for winners, and because beef heart pastrami does not suck. If you don't want to use organ meat, brisket is a common cut used for corning and pastrami. If you do use heart, you'll need to do quite a bit of trimming. There is a lot of silverskin on the outside of the heart, plus some extra inner workings you'll need to remove.

Method

1. Dissolve salt, sugar, and cure in the water, then refrigerate until brine reaches 40 degrees. Injecting or pumping the brine into the meat is ideal, using a meat syringe, but if you are not equipped for this, simply place the meat or heart into the brine and pack loosely in a nonreactive container. Place all the dry spices except the garlic into a grinder and grind them coarsely. Add to brine with garlic. Cure the meat in this brine for 3 days in the refrigerator, if you were able to inject the meat. If you did not, brine it for at least 10 days.

2. Remove the meat from the brine and rinse. Pat dry. If you're making corned beef, prepare a pot of water and bring it to a boil. Add the meat or heart and cook until the internal temperature is around 120°F. Remove and cool.

3. If you're going for pastrami, prepare a pot of water just as though you were making corned beef, but simply parboil the meat or the heart for about 5 minutes (some people skip this step, but I swear it makes better pastrami). Remove from water, then cool slightly and rub with

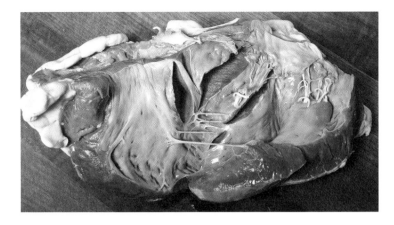

◀ An untrimmed
heart of beef

◀ Denuding the
outside of the heart

◀ Trimming the
heart's inside

the pastrami spice mixture and prepare the smoker. Wrap the meat in foil to keep moisture and spices in, then smoke until the internal temperature is 120–125°F. You want low temperatures — no higher than 200°F. Use hickory and oak or maple woods, or a blend of your own creation.

4. To serve, slice very thinly, across the grain of the meat.

LARDO

Lardo is dry cured back fat, usually served sliced thinly on an appetizer plate, or on bread. I include the recipe here so you'll have lardo for your Calabrese-Style Salami With Vanilla (page 107). Be sure to avoid light during the curing process, as light turns fat rancid. This is true of all cured meats, but when you're curing straight fat, as in the case of lardo, you'll want to be extra vigilant.

Please note Do not attempt this recipe before reading Chapter 5, which details the fermentation and curing required for finishing this preparation.

Method

1. Combine the cure ingredients and distribute evenly over the surfaces of the back fat. Place in a nonreactive bag or container and label with the date and weight. I have cured lardo in the fridge for over a year, but you can also leave it for a week before rinsing, weighing again, and hanging it in a climate-controlled charcuterie cabinet (see page 91). The lardo is finished when it has lost 40–50% of its weight.

INGREDIENTS

40 oz./2½ lb. pork back fat, trimmed of all meat and squared off

1.75 oz. salt

1 oz. cane sugar

0.2 oz. Cure #1

0.2 oz. rosemary

0.5 oz. ground black pepper

0.2 oz. ground juniper berries

TASSO HAM

INGREDIENTS

Per 5 lb. pork brisket
    or sirloin:
1.6 oz. salt
0.4 oz. cayenne pepper
1.5 oz. sweet paprika
1 oz. garlic, minced
1.5 oz. black pepper
0.2 oz. ground cinnamon
0.5 oz. ground white
    pepper
0.5 oz. brown sugar
0.2 oz. Cure #1 (optional)

Tasso is a Cajun tradition, and one of my very favorite ways to prepare pork sirloin. It also suits a pork brisket nicely, if your butcher will cut one for you — from the picnic subprimal.

Method

1. Mix all ingredients and distribute evenly over the surfaces of the meat. Weigh, label, and refrigerate 7–9 days, overhauling at even intervals. When the curing step is complete, remove from the fridge and rinse, then place in front of a box fan to dry while you prepare your smoker. Smoke tasso at temperatures no higher than 200°F, until the ham reaches an internal temperature of 145°F. Rest before slicing and serving. You can win friends (and men) with this. I have no idea how I know these things.

PORK SHANK CONFIT

INGREDIENTS

1 pork shank with or
    without trotter
1 pig tail
1 whole corm of garlic,
    with the top ¼ inch
    sliced off to expose
    all the cloves
2–3 pounds of pork fat,
    cut into cubes
1–2 Tbsp quatre épices
0.7 oz. salt

Use this recipe to confit anything (which is the preservative process of cooking and storing bone-in joints in fat). My latest interest is pork shank, trotter, and tail confit. The skin makes for great texture, and the sinewy meat of the shank lends itself well to a slow braise in fat and garlic. Use the finished product in your Chutney & Confit Terrine (page 39).

Quatre épices is French for "four spices." Make your own by combining ⅔ cup white peppercorns, 3 whole nutmegs, a heaping tablespoon of whole clove, and 3 tsp ground ginger in a sturdy spice grinder. Store in an airtight, opaque container where you keep your spices.

Method

1. Mix the salt and quatre épices and distribute over the leg and tail. You may choose to run a knife under the skin of the pork shank, just to loosen the skin slightly (don't take it all the way off!). This way you can work the salt and quatre épices into the meat more thoroughly. Place in a nonreactive bag or other container labeled with the date, for 24–48 hours.

2. When the time is up, rinse the leg and tail, pat them dry and place them in a large cast-iron skillet. Place the garlic, cut-side down, into the skillet as well. Surround everything with the pork fat, as much as you can muster. Place the skillet on the stove top over low heat, and slowly melt the fat. Preheat the oven to 300°F.

3. As the leg and tail brown slightly, and the fat begins to melt (you may choose to add a tiny bit of water to keep the fat from browning as it melts), remove the skillet from the burner and place it in the oven. Leave it until the pork leg has bent at all its joints, the bones are breaking through the skin, and the meat pulls gently off of the bone. Remove from the oven, take the garlic out to use as a special spread or pizza topping, and move the leg and tail to a ceramic crock

or other deep container, pouring the fat in around them. Allow the crock to sit and the fat to solidify. You will then store the Crock in the fridge, with the leg and tail sealed safely under the seasoned fat.

4. To serve, remove the tail and leg from the fat and warm in the oven. Flake off pieces to use in handpies, on pizza, in pasta, or in sauces. The seasoned fat can be saved for other applications, such as frying eggs or searing fish.

COPPA OR CAPICOLA

Coppa, capicola, or capocollo is made with many different muscles, but the collar muscle group is favored more widely. This is a group of four muscles in the shoulder, at the top near the neck. To cut out the coppa, start with a bone-in Boston butt, then lift the ribs and spine from the meat. You'll be able to see the coppa group pretty much right under the spinous processes (those tall, flat bones that wing off the top of the spinal column). Making sure you have all four muscles that form the round coppa, roll it off of the muscles underneath it.

Note This recipe calls for fermentation, and curing in a climate-controlled charcuterie cabinet. Read Chapter 5 before continuing.

Method

1. Mix the dry cure ingredients together and sieve if needed. Distribute the cure mix evenly over the entire surface of the coppa. Weigh, record weight, and transfer to the fridge to cure for 7–10 days, overhauling at even intervals. When salt curing is finished, rinse the coppa and set aside. Rinse a beef bung cap thoroughly, and trim to accommodate the coppa. Stuff the coppa into the beef bung by hand. Tie the end of the bung in a double knot. Using twine, tie up the coppa (see sidebar on tying for hanging and smoking, page 80). Record the weight of the coppa, then hang it up in your charcuterie cabinet, keeping it between 50-60°F and from 65-75% relative humidity until it has lost 40-50% of its weight.

> **INGREDIENTS**
> 2.5 lb. coppa cut
> 1.2 oz. kosher salt
> 0.2 oz. Cure #2
> 0.6 oz. cane sugar
> 0.5 oz. black pepper
> 0.2 oz. ground coriander
> 0.2 oz. minced garlic
> 0.1 oz. grated nutmeg
> 0.05 oz. ground cinnamon
> 0.1 oz. orange zest
> 0.1 oz. ground juniper

▲ A beef bung cap

▲ Stuffed coppa, ready for tying

◀ Finished coppa

Tying for Hanging and Smoking

Using butcher's twine, pass the twine under the top knot of your ham or coppa (or nduja, as pictured here). With the hand that is holding the bound end (the end connected to the roll of twine, pictured here in my right hand), develop a loop around your fingers.

Now, pass the loop under the free end of the string, so that it looks like a sideways capital "A."

Next, pass the free end of the string around the "legs" of the "A."

Then send the free end of the string through the "head" of the "A."

The untightened slip knot should look kind of like a pretzel.

Now you should be able to slide the knot down onto the meat, ensuring it is nice and tight.

Turn the meat around, so your slipknot is facing your belly. Extend the string out with your leading hand, and twist it to make a loop.

Twist the same loop again.

Pass the loop over the entire meat package, situating it where you want it and tightening it down by pulling on the string.

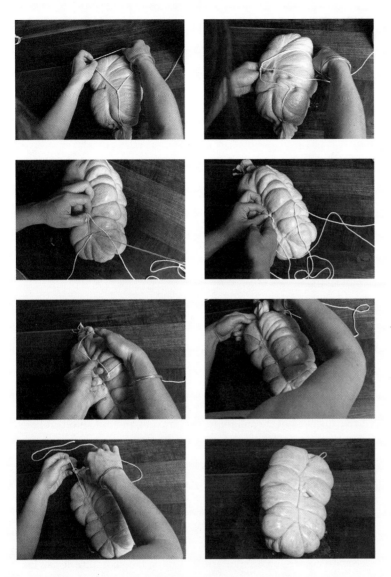

Make another loop, twist it twice, and pass it over the meat, situating it about 2 inches from the first loop, then tighten it down.

Continue making these loops and passing them over the meat, situating 2 inches apart until you have reached the end of the casing. Flip the meat over. Pass the free end of your string up underneath the back of your last loop. Then pass it under again. This will tether it to the fixed loops. You are now making your way back up to the knot at the top of the casing.

Continue looping the lead string around the fixed loops until you have made your way back to the top, where you started.

When you get to the top, send the string around the bubble knot in the casing, then pass it back under the nearest fixed loop, to the right of the central vertical string.

Pass the string over the central vertical strand, then back up under the fixed loop on the left side of the vertical strand. You'll end up with your free end facing the casing's top knot again, and you'll want to pass it around the back.

Tie a slip knot, just as you did in steps 1–5, to finish the masterpiece. Now you're ready to hang for smoking or air curing!

BLACK PEPPER CULATELLO

INGREDIENTS

6.72 oz. sea salt

2 oz. black pepper

0.48 oz. Cure #2

additional black pepper,
for use after curing

One 12-pound culatello
(if your butcher is not
familiar with this cut,
ask for the top round,
bottom round, eye of
round and knuckle all
connected together; if
you get the ball tip meat
too, that's also fine)

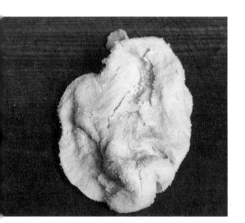

▲ A hog's bladder. Rinse and soak and get ready to stretch considerably.

Culatello is an Italian butchery term, and is the principal accepted means for obtaining a whole boneless ham in the charcuterie world. I've heard that it means "belt," although this is not a direct translation. It is a helpful insinuation, however, as cutting culatello involves unwrapping all the leg muscles from the femur bone without splitting them apart. The result is a 12–16-pound boneless ham.

Please note Do not attempt this recipe before reading Chapter 5, which details the fermentation and curing required for finishing this preparation.

Of all the things I have ever made using just salt and pepper, this culatello has made more people swoon than anything else.

Method

1. Rinse the culatello by unfurling it and running cold water over the inside and the outside of the muscles. Pat dry. Mix the cure ingredients and sieve if necessary. Distribute the cure mix evenly over all the surfaces of the culatello, both inside and out. "Roll" it back up, place in a nonreactive bag or container, weigh, and place in the refrigerator to cure. I have cured a culatello for 3 months before, but 18–20 days will do. When the time is up, rinse the culatello thoroughly, inside and out, and weigh it. Then grind up the additional black pepper, and spread it evenly over the outside of the culatello only. Stuff into a hog bladder or wrap in cheesecloth and hang in a climate-controlled charcuterie chamber, labeled, until it has lost 40–50% of its weight. I have had one culatello ready as soon as 18 months, and have left another one hanging for 2.5 years before cutting and serving.

2. To serve, unwrap and slice paper thin. To store, dust pepper over the cut end of the culatello, then re-wrap, and hang until you need it again.

Variation Make speck. Speck is a German cured ham, and one of my favorite things in the world. It is produced by salt curing a culatello, fermenting it (see Chapter 5), cold smoking it with beech wood (see Chapter 6), then hanging it up and drying it until it reaches 30–50% weight loss. You could follow the Black Pepper Culatello recipe exactly, you'd just add a cold smoking step in there, and maybe omit at least some of that black pepper. Beginners, be sure to read the next two chapters before attempting this recipe at all.

5

ON COLLABORATION

Do I contradict myself?
Very well then I contradict myself,
(I am large, I contain multitudes.)
WALT WHITMAN *Song of Myself* (1855)

AT THE HEART of charcuterie practice is dynamic collaboration with nature and her infinite mysteries and possibilities. Embedded into every inch of dynamism that we can see with the naked eye, from the soil under the pig's feet to the feed stuffs, to the muscle and the fat and the earth-made salt, there are unseen forces colluding. Microscopic forces. Bacteria, fungi, protozoa, and other microorganisms, and interactions between them, are crucial players in creating an excellent product, chiefly as they exist in the soil, which supports animals in life, and also as they exist in the fermenting meat on its way to cured perfection. In this way, curing meats truly punctuates a full-circle craft. I think this is one of my favorite things about charcuterie — the microorganisms, and the fact that they are the clear main players at the very beginning and the very end of a well-hewn process. This is some kind of sweet extra knowledge that settles my art neatly into form.

What happens to a piece of meat that is never cooked, once it has been salt cured and seasoned? What makes it possible for us

▲ From left to right: prosciutto, coppa, pancetta, culatello

to safely consume such a product, and preserve it without refrigeration? The answer is fermentation, and a sister process we refer to as "drying," though that word hardly seems to do it justice. That's because both fermentation and "drying" in the sense of "completing the cure" don't simply refer to dehydration, but also to a biological process informed by none other than microorganisms.

Fermentation is the metabolic process by which sugars, both simple and complex, are metabolized by microorganisms into lactic acids and alcohols. It doesn't matter if you are making sauerkraut, yogurt, wine or salami, this is the process you are working with, and for its success, you will depend largely on two chief genera of bacteria: *Lactobacillus* and *Pediococcus*. As you craft a lomo (page 112) or a Calabrese Salami (page 107), you will provide a proper

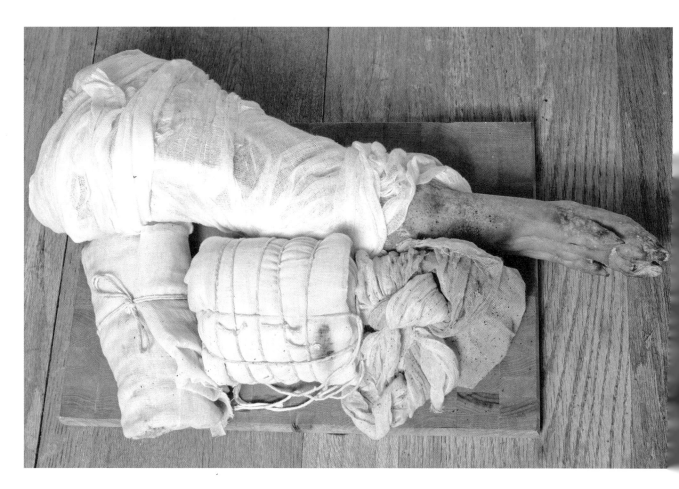

environment and food for these bacteria, both in the complex sugars naturally present in the meat, and in added sugars that you include in the recipe. Temperature and sugar content are the chief drivers of their activity. (The hotter and sweeter it is, the faster they work, and the more drastic their effect on flavor.) Depending on quantity, added sugars can be included simply to fuel fermenting bacteria, or to add sweetness during the eating experience. These bacteria consume the sugars, breaking them down to produce alcohols and acids, which accomplishes two notable things: 1) It produces the sourly flavor that we associate with fermented food products, and 2) It lowers the pH (relative acidity) of the product, thereby making it inhospitable to harmful organisms and attractive to other genera of bacteria that will continue the work of dehydration and curing.

This is where the dynamism gets even more mind-blowing. When the fermentation bacteria begin to run out of sugar, they start to die. In my imagination, this used to consist of a slow fading of productivity and a decline in population, almost like the fade to white or fuzz at the end of a good tune. Then I would picture the beneficial "finisher" bacteria, the *Staphylococcus* and *Kocuria* genera, coming in gradually, like a rising sun, slowly going about the work of flavoring, coloring, and completing the cured product by interacting with the proteins in the meat, and with nitrite. And while this is somewhat correct, it is too tidy a picture, and doesn't convey the fiery side of the transition. It turns out that when those fermenting critters approach the end of their tenure, they might actually explode, over-stuffed, and the enzymatic soup of their fantastic deaths is just as much responsible for the flavor we experience as is the work of their "finisher" bacteria symbionts. Isn't that fascinating, and fine? Again, nature offers us a supreme example of the utility in death, and the partnership between death and life. The parallel between the life and death of domesticated livestock, and the life and death of the incredible microorganisms that allow for sustainable preservation, is too beautiful to ignore.

Finally, an understanding of the science of the microorganisms behind charcuterie gives us further support for the case for pure charcuterie. Mass-produced cured meats have been designed to fit with the system of mechanized food production, with quick turnarounds and cheap prices. The industry simply can't afford to foster pure curing techniques, because they take too long. Old World flavors and pure technique require patience and simplicity, allowing nature to work her magic. If you are concerned with producing a high volume of salami as fast as you possibly can, you will be required to pump it with human-isolated strains of bacteria to ensure inoculation. You will be tempted to add far too much sweetener, and kick temperatures up very high to speed fermentation reactions. Fast fermentation produces too sour a product for sale, prompting you to add more sweeteners. And, to get the product off the line even faster, you'll cut short the work of the finisher microorganisms by adding synthetic stabilizers, coloring agents, and other preservatives in their stead.

Armed with this knowledge, you now know that you will never, ever be able to get the real thing from the supermarket. You won't get the flavor or the character, and you won't get the purity of something you can make at home. Furthermore, any claims you have heard about cured meats posing a threat to your health should be attributed to the products that dominate mainstream outlets — mass-produced cured meats, pumped full of genetically modified sweeteners, preservatives, colorants, and more. Making your own deli meats and salamis at home, using clean ingredients, enjoyment for the process, and patience toward the outcome poses few negatives to your system. I assure you it will enrich your life, your plate, and your view on the world, as you welcome some of the most fascinating work of nature into your home kitchen.

You're already familiar with salt curing, which we covered in the last chapter, so what comes next? For those preparations from Chapter 4 such as lardo and culatello, as well as a host of new recipes in this chapter, you'll learn next to collaborate with microbes to ferment and dry your salt-cured projects. In addition, we will cover fermented dry sausages, taking your sausage-making and suspensions skills to another dimension. Lastly, we will discuss creating a climate-controlled charcuterie cabinet for fermentation and curing, and using *starter cultures* and *beneficial molds* to better ferment and preserve your meat products.

FERMENTED DRY SAUSAGES

The process for making dry sausages isn't much different from the process for making fresh sausages and suspensions, which you learned in Chapters 2 and 3. The difference, as you might have guessed, lies in the ratios of the recipe. Additionally, while fresh sausages don't include a nitrate or a curing step, many dry sausages

and salamis do. As such, we won't spend a lot of time talking about mixing and grinding. You can refer to the specific recipes for details on that, and the sausage-making primer in Chapter 2. The best advice I can give you on crafting fermented dry sausages lies in ratio adjustment.

Ground meats destined for fermentation and never intended for cooking are considered some of the most difficult preparations within the charcuterie realm, simply because they are the most susceptible to contamination. Think about it — if ground meat has the most surface area, and you're going to put it through a series of processes right around room temperature, without ever intending to cook it, it seems like a ripe breeding ground for pathogens, no? Remember, though, that the good microorganisms are easier to encourage than the bad ones. Considering this, salt content must absolutely go up in the production of fermented dry sausages. Our aim is to create an environment that is salty enough to be inhospitable to harmful microorganisms without creating an overly salty food product. The ratio for achieving this balance is a salt content between 2.5–3.5% of the weight of the meat. Spices and liquids will mirror what you've learned in fresh sausage making or suspensions work, for the most part, although you may find that added liquid is rarer in fermented preparations.

As for meat-to-fat ratios, this varies considerably in the world of dry sausages. Pepperoni, for example, is traditionally a very lean product, and some recipes, including my own, call for no added fat whatsoever, just lean beef and lean pork in even quantities. Many salamis are set at an 80:20 lean to fat ratio, and some are 90:10. For nduja, which you will learn about on page 108, you're looking at 60% fat, and only 40% lean! The point is, tradition and texture rule the day on lean:fat in fermented products. If you are setting out to create your own recipes, start with 80:20 and see what you like from there.

An important ingredient in dry sausages is sodium nitrate (Cure #2). This is a more complex form of nitrogen than Cure #1, and allows for a slow-release reaction of sodium nitrite, which will interact with microorganisms to inhibit botulism. Cure #2 is used for longer-curing items, while Cure #1 is used for cooked or quicker preparations. This is added according to regulated amounts, as discussed in Chapter 4.

In general, once you've tweaked these things within the ratio, you'll mix and grind according to textural desires, just as you do for fresh sausages. Then, you may consider letting the ground mixture sit, refrigerated, for anywhere from 8 to 48 hours. This increases bind, and allows flavors to meld while the mix cures. After this step, you can go on to stuffing and pricking the salamis all over. And I mean all over. Use a sterilized tack or needle or a clean sausage pricker. This prevents air pockets from forming under the casing as water activity decreases and the meat mass shrinks. In all the charcuterie classes I've taught, this is the step most often missed or underperformed by participants, and it can lead to case hardening (drying of the casing before the meat) and mold pockets.

Next, you'll hang the salamis in your charcuterie chamber. You'll notice that the humidity and temperature will naturally rise as fermentation happens, and then as drying and curing begins the cabinet will mellow to a temperature and humidity closer to the settings you have designated. This is because initially, the moisture in the raw meat is high, kicking up the humidity, and because the activity of the fermenting microbes creates heat and energy. As water activity decreases and fermenters die, the environment will change noticeably.

With the above in mind, the purest of salamis and fermented sausages can be made at home. While you'll hear tales of extra acidifiers, colorants and preservatives, I assure you I have made a creative diversity of delicious dry sausages without them. I'd gently urge you to do the same, and keep it pure.

MAKING A CHARCUTERIE CABINET

Crafting the recipe is half the battle; the other half is providing the environment for food preservation. Charcuterie cabinets are controlled environments allowing us to control temperature and humidity to an optimum range for our desired purposes. Very generally speaking, a dark environment at about 50–60°F and around 65–75% relative humidity will get the job done. If you have a root cellar, it will likely work, and I myself have discovered pockets in my house and corners in my basement that work as well. If you'd like to make an official cabinet, all you need is an insulated box with an external thermostat and humidistat. I use a refrigerator, and have wired an external digital thermostat into it that will override the refrigerator's normal temperature controls. The external digital thermostat is set between 50 and 60 degrees Fahrenheit. I have two fans inside the cabinet to promote air circulation. I also have a cool

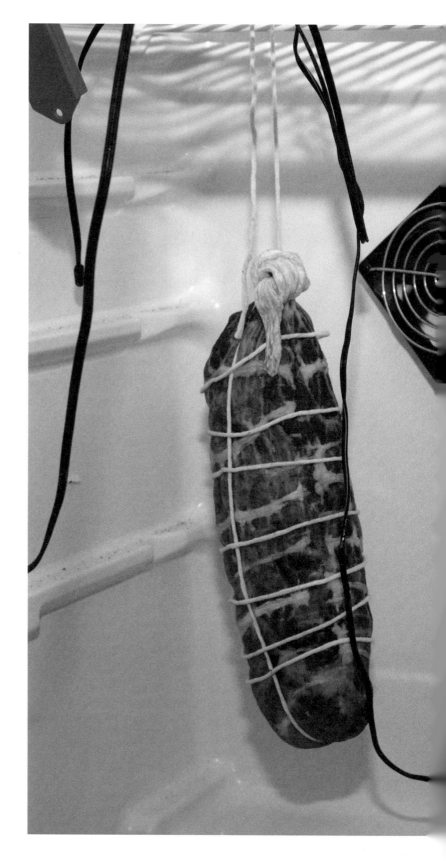

▶ Meats hanging in converted refrigerator charcuterie cabinet

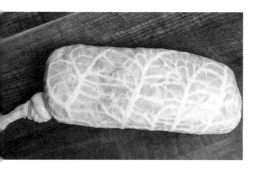

▲ This coppa has just been stuffed and is ready to hang.

▲ The same coppa is smaller a month later, after it has undergone some fermentation and curing. It is still not finished curing here.

mist humidifier wired into an external humidistat, set to regulate the relative humidity between 65–75%.

The simplest way to do this is to get your hands on an old fridge (don't use a side-by-side, it's a waste of space). Go online and buy an external thermostat with a three-prong outlet on it. This will cost you about $100. Buy an external humidistat with an outlet on it. Plug the fridge into the thermostat, and plug a cool mist humidifier (about $40) into the humidistat. For about $250, you've got yourself a decent curing chamber. You will probably want a desk fan inside the cabinet to promote airflow, if humidity gets too high.

If you want instructions for hard wiring your fridge into an external thermostat, and hard wiring your humidifier into an external humidistat, check out my first book, *The Ethical Meat Handbook*.

Once you've got this little microclimate established, you're ready to start concocting salamis, lomo, coppa, guanciale, and a host of other preserved meat products. You'll hang these items up once they have salt cured and been stuffed or wrapped, and tied. Then let the microorganisms go to work. You'll know the product is ready when it has lost 40–50% of its weight.

During the fermentation and drying process, you will notice considerable weight loss and shrinkage as the meat loses water activity. This is why you want to make sure your knots are extra tight!

STARTER CULTURES AND BENEFICIAL MOLDS

Starter cultures are isolated strains or combined isolated strains of beneficial microorganisms, produced by the food industry for inoculating cured meats. If you're not familiar with the process of inoculation, it simply refers to the addition of beneficial microorganisms to a substrate, to ensure proper biological processes over time. Pea seeds, which fix nitrogen in the soil, have a specific bacterial symbiont, and gardeners and farmers can purchase dried bacterial cultures to use in inoculating their seed. Similarly, bacteria that will ferment and cure meat products are isolated into several standard starter cultures that can be added to ground meat mixtures to ensure proper preservation.

Personally, I do not love using isolated starter cultures, as they are a product of an industry I am not fond of supporting, and I'm in favor of promoting processing which encourages the proper bacterial strains to present themselves in the meat products naturally. Because fermenter bacteria are ubiquitous, it is reasonable to believe that without any added starter culture, home practitioners can expect proper fermentation and curing. That said, many producers use them, and for beginners it is an extra assurance that you've got the good guys working for you. If you choose not to use them, at least understand their purpose as you begin your charcuterie craft. If you do use them, I encourage you to experiment without them as you gain confidence in your gauge of food safety and the proper scientific processes at hand in your charcuterie cabinet. Indeed, many salumists are some of the most accomplished experimenters I know. What will happen if I put macaroni in salami? Only one way to find out….

▲ Close-up of *Penicillium nalgiovense* coverage on a salami

For all of the uncooked or long-fermented recipes in this book, I have included T-SPX starter culture as an ingredient. This is by far my go-to of all the starters, as it is the choice for slower, more traditional-styled curing projects. Similar cultures to T-SPX are T-RM-F3 and T-SP. Other commonly used starter cultures are F-RM-52, which is used for faster fermentation and higher temperatures, and F-LC, which works at different time and temperature settings but also includes a kind of antibiotic that prevents listeria from exceeding safe levels. The list of all available cultures is long, and their uses vary based on process and intent. I assure you that if you are committed to Pure Charcuterie, that is charcuterie with pure ingredients and traditional processes, you need not possess a deep and complex understanding of all the commercially available strains and their unique properties. T-SPX and its brethren will get you off to a fine start with plenty of beneficial lactobacillus species and no need to tweak other ingredients or climate controls too much.

A beneficial mold that you will become familiar with in producing fermented sausages is *Penicillium nalgiovense*, which is the white mold you have no doubt seen on the surface of many salami products. *P. nalgiovense* is a fungus, just like all molds, and comes in a few forms, each of which is more effective at specific temperature ranges and relative humidity levels. M-EK-72, M-EK-4, and M-EK-6 will all give you the white mold, but M-EK-4 works at lower temperatures and lower relative humidity, producing a less fuzzy mold. The other two work at higher temperatures and humidity levels, and will produce a thicker, fluffier coverage. As you start out, any of the three *P. nalgiovense* strains will work for your purposes, which are mostly to ensure there is a beneficial mold on the surface of your salamis that is aggressive enough to outcompete any other surface molds that might produce off-flavors in the final product. In general, surface molds that can populate the outside of a casing are not hazardous to your health — they just don't lend the right flavor, so you want to avoid them by keeping humidity in the proper ranges (see Making a Charcuterie Cabinet, above), and by using penicillium to work in your favor.

I like to generate my own penicillium. Do this by letting an organic orange sit out and grow white mold that turns to an olive green, then scraping it off and diluting it in a spray bottle. Or I pull the casing off of salami that I have inoculated with penicillium and soak it in a bottle of lukewarm water before spraying the water on finished salamis that are ready to go into the cabinet. I also usually keep a package of M-EK-72 in the freezer just in case. Cultures will keep for some time in the freezer, so if you want to get some just to have on hand it isn't a bad idea.

The other mold with exciting applications in the charcuterie world is *Aspergillus oryzae*, otherwise known as koji. The amazing thing about this mold, which has been used for centuries to make miso, sake and soy sauce, is that it ferments and cures kind of in tandem, and its applications for curing meat are very exciting indeed.

KOJI CHARCUTERIE

Koji charcuterie is a method of preserving meat that relies on *Aspergillus oryzae*, or koji mold, grown directly on the surface of the meat. This mold is a filamental fungus (as is *P. nalgiovense*), which might seem weird, since most people think of fungus as a typical Mario Brothers mushroom. The truth is that fungi come in many shapes, sizes and colors, and the "mushroom" you picture is just the fruiting body of the dynamic fungus — its way of getting its "seed" out to the world. If you think about it, this isn't too crazy. The familiar apple, for example, is really just an ovary, holding the seed of the apple tree. Likewise, there is more to fungus than its fruiting body. What more? Well, the mycelium, which you can think of as the fungus's "roots." Mycelia are highly networked, forming mats and webs, and are responsible for incredibly dynamic metabolic activity in the life of any fungus. Understanding this may help you recognize surface molds such as penicillium and koji as fungi indeed. In warm, moist environments rich in oxygen, koji can grow on the surface of nearly anything, and what you'll see is a literal mat of filamental white, yellow or pale-green mycelia, growing all over the substrate. I've heard of koji mold being used to break down plastic (seriously), and using the same metabolism, it can work its magic on meat as well.

The science of how koji works is a bit more complex than we have room to explore, but the main thing to understand is that its mycelial mat produces many enzymes, which work to break big molecules into smaller ones. The bigger molecules we're talking about here are starches, carbohydrates, proteins and fats, and they are being reduced to simpler sugars, amino acids, fatty acid chains, etc. With what you know about fermentation and curing so far, you might be able to guess that these smaller molecules are prime nutrition for some other microorganisms (like our friend *Lactobacillus*), and in this way, koji lays a spectacular groundwork for natural fermentation processes to unfold. But, in tandem with other microbes, koji's enzymes have their own added effects. For example, it has been found that typically tough cuts of meat can be cultured with koji spores; once the koji populates their surface and releases its enzymes into the meat, it radically tenderizes the cuts. Additionally, meat that is cured using koji has been shown to cure in at least a third of the time that meat cures using traditional charcuterie practice, due to the ongoing activity of koji's enzymes during the curing process. It's truly amazing.

I'm not an expert on koji charcuterie, and have only recently been introduced to the power of koji across all of its applications, from miso to soy sauce to sake and vinegars. I'm extremely excited about the applications, however, and am now happily growing koji like a fiend, right next to my desk. I grow it on everything from rice to barley to pork loins, after the advice of Chef Jeremy Umansky, the leader in koji charcuterie, using methods he developed at his restaurant in Ohio. Chef Umansky has contributed his own recipe to this chapter, so you can get a sense of how the experts are working with koji and meat. I've also included my own koji experiment, a recipe I am developing for a local restaurant here in Asheville, NC. Umansky is working on his own books and is totally open-sourcing his projects online. Do yourself a favor and check out his restaurant, Larder, and the social media associated with the exciting work he is doing.

GROWING KOJI

Like any mold, koji prefers warmth and moisture. Temperatures of roughly 80–95 degrees Fahrenheit and high humidity levels are ideal for koji to thrive. Since this is decidedly not the ideal environment for your home, you'll have to rig up a small incubator for your koji projects. My incubator is made from a 12-x-24-inch plastic tub about 6 inches deep, with a lid. I fill it about a third of the way with water, and in that water I place a roughly $40 aquarium heater, capable of heating water up to 90 degrees. You can find these anywhere they sell tropical fish. The aquarium thermometer is plugged into the wall beside my desk, and then run into the water and suctioned to the bottom of the plastic bin. I crank it all the way up to 88 degrees,

▲ Koji culture on barley after 16 hours

then invert a couple of small loaf pans in the water, allowing me to place a 9-×-13-inch glass casserole pan on top of them so that the casserole pan is submerged in the water but not loosely floating. Then whatever I am koji culturing can hang out in the casserole pan, covered in a towel, and happily form sweetly fragrant koji mold on its surface. I typically cover whatever I am culturing in a tea towel, which I change out daily. This prevents any condensation from dripping consistently on the food. While koji likes high humidity, I find that it helps to keep whatever you are culturing from getting downright soaked.

So, how do you get the koji on there to begin with? The answer is, you'll need to buy a starter culture. I know I kind of scoffed at this

▲ Close-up of *Aspergillus oryzae*, or koji mold

earlier, but it is important to understand that koji is relatively difficult to conjure from the wild. Research into ancient Asian methods for doing this show they involve making strange cake-like concoctions from as many as twenty different native wild plants, and allowing these to ferment wrapped in leaves until the mycelial mat forms on their surface. Assuming you don't have the flora of a Chinese mountainside at your disposal, it is best to start by buying koji spores from reputable independent sources. My favorite provider is GEM Cultures. There are several types of koji, and they are grown on different grains. My favorite is barley koji, but you can choose what you want. Once you've picked it out, it will be mailed to you in a little bag with instructions for use. It looks like olive green powder.

I like to do about 4 cups of organic pearled barley at a time. That's about 2 pounds. The package instructions may suggest to soak or rinse the barley, but Jeremy says not to do either, as koji is a saccharifying mold, meaning it seeks out starch and breaks it down. So the more starch, the better. Steam the barley. I use a bamboo steamer for about 45 minutes, until it is cooked and sticky. After cooking, I'll turn it out onto a towel and break up the clumps, allowing it to cool slightly. Jeremy suggests temping it during the cooling process, aiming for 90°F. While it is cooling, I toast about ¼ cup of flour in a cast iron skillet, to sanitize it, then mix it with about 2 tsp of koji spores. If I am using koji from a previous batch, I'll use double this amount, simply because part of the barley from the last batch is in there as dry matter, and it isn't straight koji spores that I'm adding to the mix.

Once you've mixed the toasted flour with the koji spores, you're ready to add them to the cooked barley. I usually sprinkle about half of the flour and koji mix onto the barley, then mix it around with my hands. It should smell good, like a meadow wildflower. Once I've moved it around to coat the grains as much as possible, I'll sprinkle the rest of the flour/koji mix on and combine again, using my hands. After all the mixing, I bundle the koji up into the towel, leaving a slight opening at the top. Then I'll put the bundle into my casserole dish and place the dish into the incubator, close the lid and leave it alone for a bit.

I like to check the temperature of my koji every few hours. It will take 36–40 hours at 88–90 degrees before the barley gets its fluffy white mycelial mat. For the first 24 hours, I keep the barley bundled in the towel, temping it with a meat thermometer every few hours to ensure it is keeping around 85–90 degrees. After 24 hours in the towel, I pull it out and dump the barley directly into the casserole pan, spreading it into an even layer. At this point, you may want to make a couple of furrows in the barley, to prevent the mix from overheating. Cover the pan with a towel and put it back in the incubator;

then when you check the temperature every few hours, you can move the furrows to different places.

What you are watching for is a thick, fluffy, white or slightly yellow coverage of mold. After about 24 hours it will look lightly dusted, and after 36–48 hours you will see the thicker coverage. Leaving the koji to incubate longer will cause it to mature to the point where it wants to produce spores. You can tell this is happening if the mold begins to turn olive green. If you want to use it for miso or sake, try to harvest it before it gets to this point. If it does start to turn green, that's OK. You can still harvest it and use it to seed a future batch of grain.

To harvest, just pull the barley from the incubator and spread it out to let it dry and cool, then put it into a nonreactive container and store it in the fridge. Most recipes that use koji to ferment will have you pulverize the barley with the mold on it before adding it to other ingredients.

So what does all this have to do with meat, again? Well, now that you know how to grow koji on grain, you simply use the same principles to grow koji on meat. I'm not even kidding. The first time I did this, I was absolutely sure it was going to rot, but it didn't. The process is outlined in more detail in the two recipes for koji charcuterie included in this chapter, but the basic process is to salt cure the meat, adding any other flavorings you want, just as you normally would (see Chapter 4 for details on salt curing, if you need to brush up on this). After the meat has cured in salt, you'll dust it with a flour/koji mix just as the barley was, and then place it in the casserole pan in the koji incubator. It might seem incredibly wrong to be putting a piece of meat into a 90-degree bin, but trust me, it works. The koji will colonize the meat's surface, and when you're satisfied with the mold growth you see, it's time to weigh the meat, record the weight, and then hang it in your charcuterie cabinet. It will hang there until it has lost 40–50% of its weight. Jeremy's work over the last two years has shown that it will reach this finished weight in drastically less time than a piece of meat you've simply salt cured and hung to dry.

With all this info at your fingertips, you may well ask, Why do anything BUT koji charcuterie? Well, to that I have a few answers. First and foremost, koji has its own complex and distinctive flavors, and just as you wouldn't want every cured meat project to include anise or paprika, you may not want every project to include koji. Additionally, it may outcompete other microbes that you'd like to favor, so doing projects without koji from time to time can enrich diversity in your cabinet and your biological arsenal. That being said, koji is addictive. I won't lie. The first time you smell its sweetness, you may be inclined to disagree with me.

CHILE, MUSTARD &
PICKLED CELERY SALAMI

INGREDIENTS

4 lb. pork lean trim (80%)

1 lb. pork back fat (20%)

2.5 oz. salt

0.2 oz. Cure #2

1.6 oz. organic dextrose

0.5 oz. black pepper

1.5 oz. pickled celery leaves,
    minced (See page 128)

0.3 oz. ground guajillo
    chile pepper

0.2 oz. onion powder

0.1 oz. ground mustard

0.5 oz. minced garlic

T-SPX starter culture

1 cup red wine

12–14 feet of beef middle
    casings

Penicillium nalgiovense
    culture

This is the craziest thing I have ever made. It blooms on your tongue with layers of umami, and is truly unlike any other salami I have ever had.

Method

1. Mix about 2 tsp of the starter culture into ¼ cup of room-temperature water. Set aside.

2. Combine the lean trim with all the seasonings and grind through the fine die of your meat grinder. Set aside. Next, grind the fat through the coarse die of your meat grinder. Combine the lean meat mixture with the fat, using your gloved hands, then add in the wine and the starter culture. Mix with your hands or in a stand mixer for at least a minute, then transfer the entire mixture to the refrigerator for 24 hours. This will increase bind and meld flavor.

3. The next day, prepare beef middle casings and stuff the salami mixture into them, stopping every foot to 18 inches and tying off the ends. Link each 12–18-inch sausage in the middle, to form two salamis, each 6–9 inches long. Tie twine at each end and in between the links. Prick the salamis thoroughly, then weigh them and record their weight.

4. Spray the salamis with *Penicillium nalgiovense*, diluted according to package instructions.

5. Hang to ferment and dry, aiming at 60–65 degrees and 65–75% humidity. Don't worry if humidity increases at first, while fermentation is happening. The salami is done when it has lost 30–40% of its starting weight.

CALABRESE-STYLE SALAMI
WITH VANILLA & LARDO

This salami is beautiful, sweet, and mild. A crowd-pleaser and a kid-pleaser. You'll find the ratio of salt decreased slightly to account for the saltiness of the lardo.

Method

1. Mix about 2 tsp of the starter culture into ¼ cup of room-temperature water. Set aside.

2. Combine the lean trim and the pound of back fat with all the seasonings and grind through the fine die of your meat grinder. Set aside. Combine the lean meat mixture with the cubed fat, using your gloved hands, then add in the wine and the starter culture. Mix with your hands or in a stand mixer for at least a minute, then transfer the entire mixture to the refrigerator for 24 hours. This will increase bind and meld flavor.

3. The next day, prepare beef middle casings and stuff the salami mixture into them, stopping every foot to 18 inches and tying off the ends. Link each 12–18-inch sausage in the middle, to form two salamis, each 6–9 inches long. Tie twine at each end and in between the links. Prick the salamis thoroughly, then weigh them and record their weight.

4. Spray the salamis with *Penicillium nalgiovense*, diluted according to package instructions.

5. Hang to ferment and dry, aiming at 60–65 degrees and 65–75% humidity. Don't worry if humidity increases at first, while fermentation is happening. The salami is done when it has lost 30–40% of its starting weight.

INGREDIENTS

4 lb. pork lean trim

1 lb. pork back fat

1 lb. cured lardo, cubed into ¼-inch pieces (see page 73)

2 oz. salt

0.2 oz. Cure #2

1.6 oz. dextrose

0.2 oz. black pepper, ground

0.3 oz. white pepper, ground

0.2 oz. anise seed, ground

¼ cup white wine

0.1 oz. cinnamon, ground

0.2 oz. pure vanilla extract (I make my own by steeping vanilla beans in Kentucky bourbon)

0.5 oz. garlic

T-SPX

12–14 ft beef middle casings

Penicillium nalgiovense culture

NDUJA

INGREDIENTS

5 lb. of pork jowl, trimmed
to 1-x-3-inch strips

Or

3 lb. pork fat (60%)

2 lb. pork lean trim (40%)

Plus

2.2 oz. salt

0.2 oz. Cure #2

0.32 oz. organic dextrose

16 oz. Calabrian chilies in
oil, or any mix of hot
& sweet peppers from
your garden

T-SPX

1 hog bung, also called
a hog middle cap

Nduja is a meaty adventure, from its spice to its texture to its complex processing. As such, it is for the more adventurous salumists. It is spreadable salami traditionally made with pork jowl, and aside from smearing it on breads, it is useful for adding to sauces, broths, brown butters and roux. To be quite honest, this application was what got my imagination running wild, and compelled me to make it in the first place. Pronounce it IN-DOO-YA.

Method

1. Rinse the hog bung thoroughly and allow it to soak.

2. Freeze your grinder parts and your bowl. Mix the peppers with the jowl trim and open-freeze.

3. Mix about 2 tsp of the starter culture into ¼ cup of room temperature water. Set aside.

4. Grind the meat and pepper mixture twice through the coarse plate and twice through the fine plate. It will be very stiff. You may need to stop and chill the mix in between grinder plates, if you find it is rising above 40°F. Combine the salt, curing salt, and dextrose and sieve to remove any clumps. Put the meat mixture in your stand mixer with the paddle attachment and dump the salt mixture in. Add the T-SPX. Mix on low for 3–4 minutes while you wash your grinder parts.

5. At this point you can stop and chill the meat mix overnight, but it isn't necessary. When you are ready to stuff, place the largest stuffing horn onto your stuffer and begin to stuff the hog bung as well as you can. The way the bung is built, you'll notice many chambers, so stuffing requires a watchful attitude (see sidebar, page 110). Once you've stuffed all the meat in, tie the opening of the bung with the slip knot, then tie according to the instructions in the sidebar on page 80. You can use this same technique for tying roasts, salamis, coppa, or any other meat product.

▲ Nduja, ready for tying

6. Hang the stuffed nduja to ferment for 36–48 hours at 80–90°F and about 90–95% relative humidity. After this time, remove the nduja from the cabinet and cold smoke it (smoke at temperatures less than 80°F; see Chapter 6 for more info on smoking) for 3–4 hours. After smoking, allow to rest slightly, then return to the charcuterie cabinet to cure.

7. It is helpful to have a pH meter to determine when nduja is safe to consume, as weight loss is not as reliable a marker for this product. The pH should be 4.2–5.0. I have had nduja ready after 3 months of aging, after it has cold smoked. Hana is the most reliable producer of pH meters; see the Resources section for links.

Stuffing Large Sausages

For nduja, mortadella, and other recipes that require stuffing ground meat into a large casing or bung, here is the technique:

- Load the entire length of the casing onto the horn, so that the tied or closed end is flush with the end of the stuffing horn.
- Begin turning the crank, and let the casing fill slowly.
- Keep a firm hold on the casing as it fills, to ensure you are packing the meat mixture in as tightly as you can. Stop if you must, and distribute the ground meat as needed with your hands, to ensure it is filling the casing completely.
- When you've stuffed as much as will fit with room to tie off, or if you've run out of meat mixture, remove the casing from the stuffing horn while introducing as little air as possible into the sausage. Tie off with twine or a bubble knot.

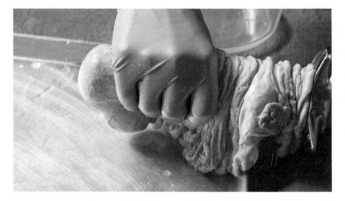

▲ A hog bung, loaded completely onto the stuffing horn

KOJI VENISON BRESAOLA

RECIPE COURTESY CHEF JEREMY
UMANSKY, LARDER, CLEVELAND, OH

Method

1. Grind all cure ingredients in a spice grinder and generously apply the cure mixture to the meat. Vacuum seal the meat and allow it to cure, in the refrigerator, for 5–10 days. Remove the meat from its packaging and place in a large bowl. Be sure to include any of the purge that accumulated during the curing time, as it will help the koji adhere to the meat.

2. In a separate bowl, mix the rice flour and spores together. Heavily dredge the cured meat with the flour.

3. Weigh the dredged meat and record. Place the meat in your koji incubator, and culture at 85°F and 90–95% relative humidity for 48 hours, or until the koji is clearly established. It will appear stark white and have a downy texture.

4. Hang the meat in your charcuterie cabinet at 50°F and 65% relative humidity until it loses 35% of its weight. Slice thinly to serve.

INGREDIENTS

2.2 lbs. venison top round (from the outside of the leg)

CURE

0.08 oz. Cure #1

0.7 oz. sea salt

0.5 oz. turbinado sugar

0.35 oz. dark cocoa powder

0.35 oz. ground coffee

0.35 oz. dried chaga mushroom, powdered

0.25 oz. dried chili flake

0.1 oz. ground cinnamon

CULTURE

3.5 oz. brown rice flour

0.5 oz. dispersed koji spores

FIVE-SPICE KOJI LOMO

INGREDIENTS

5 lb. Danish cut pork loin
  (boneless, with skin on)

CURE

3.5 oz. sea salt
1.75 oz. Chinese five spice
0.2 oz. Cure #2

CULTURE

2 oz. flour
0.5 oz. dispersed koji spores

HOMEMADE
CHINESE FIVE SPICE

6 tsp ground cinnamon
6 tsp crushed anise
1.5 tsp crushed fennel seed
1.5 tsp fresh ground black
  pepper
¾ tsp ground clove

Method

1. Combine all five spice ingredients and grind together well. Store in a cool place in an opaque bottle.

2. Combine all the cure ingredients and use half of the cure mixture to cover the surface of the loin. Seal and cure in the refrigerator for 9 days, then remove and add the remaining cure mixture to the loin. Seal again and cure for another 9 days, overhauling at even intervals.

3. Remove the lomo from the cure and place in a bowl. In a separate bowl, mix the koji spores and the flour, then cover the meat generously with the flour mixture. Culture in your koji incubator at 85-88°F and 90-95% relative humidity for 48 hours, or until the koji is established.

4. Hang the loin in your charcuterie cabinet at 50-60°F and 65% relative humidity until it has lost 40-50% of its weight. Slice thinly to serve.

6

ON CULMINATION

A woman opens a window — here and here
and here —
placing a vase of blue flowers
on an orange cloth. I follow her.
She is making soup from what she had left
in the bowl, the shriveled garlic and bent bean.
She is leaving nothing out.

NAOMI SHIHAB NYE *Half-and-Half* (1994)

WHAT IS MADE of a farmer's work, the animal's life, or the butcher's thrift, if we do not finish the piece, and finish it well? It is forgotten, as we have seen, in seventy or more years of industrialization and monopolization, of blandification and additive addiction. The essence of the life that made the food that makes us alive is snuffed out. As it deadens, we deaden. As you craft real food, food that brings you back in touch with the truth of life and death in their poetic, fragrant, and useful dance, you must strive for a finished product that is surprising, exhilarating, substantive. Right. As I carefully waxed philosophical and parsed through processes for the grinding, mixing, seasoning, salt curing, fermenting and drying of meats in this volume, my inner voice has itched to sew it up

▲ On left, Miso & Pickled Ginger Sausage. On right, Rabbit Andouille.

roundly. If we must take the craft apart to understand it, we must, at some point, put it back together, to truly see it for what it is.

COOKING SAUSAGES

You've made the fresh sausage, so how shall you cook it? The absolute best way to is to poach it first (that's cooking in water under boiling temperature, around 170°F) and then sear it off in a hot pan or on the grill to brown the outside. This method prevents you from overcooking the outside of the sausage while you're waiting for it to cook through. It also has the added advantage of allowing you to poach, save in the fridge, and then quickly cook off on the stove or grill later. Other cooking methods include smoking (see below) or baking. Baking sausages is usually reserved for recipes that call for combining them with other ingredients, and generally some added moisture is advised.

SMOKING MEAT

Smoking foods, working with fire and wood, is an entirely exhilarating realm, and I trust that anyone who dabbles in the practice of flavoring, cooking, or merely drying meats, cheeses or vegetables with wood smoke will find themselves slowly and subconsciously tantalized by the challenge of patience and balance it evokes. Some skills in smoking are essential to a full-scale charcuterie practice, the most sacred being cold smoking, which is chiefly a form of preservation and not a form of cooking.

Smoking is not barbequing, though barbequed food can be, and most often is, smoked. Smoking is not the same as grilling. Wood smoke has antioxidant properties, antimicrobial properties, and a low pH, so it is a preservative. Properly there are three types of smoke: cold, warm and hot.

Cold smoking is applying light, intermittent smoke to a food at temperatures between 68–80°F in the smoking chamber. This almost always requires indirect heat, as in, the fire located away from the meat itself. The smoke from that fire is directed toward a separate chamber, where the meat hangs or rests. Cold smoking is associated with long smoking times, although the smoke need not be constant. Cold smoking woods are beech, alder and birch.

Warm smoking is achieved by applying intermittent smoke, using either indirect or direct heat, with temperatures ranging between 80°F and 140°F in the smoke chamber. The food is sometimes cooked as it is smoked, but this is variable. Warm smoking woods are woods like apple, maple and pecan.

Hot smoking is almost always achieved with direct heat (the smoldering fire is close to or right under the meat), thicker, consistent smoke, and temperatures from 140°F to 200°F in the smoke chamber. The smoking time is almost always determined by how long it takes the food to cook, as cooking to temperature is always possible with hot smoke. Hot smoking woods are hickory, oak and mesquite. I hot smoke using my Big Green Egg ceramic grill, and have also achieved hot smoking on CharGriller and Weber grills.

Cold smoke is special in the realm of charcuterie, and in food preservation in general, for several reasons: 1) Cold smoke is relatively low maintenance. There need not be smoke on the food at all times. If the fire goes out, its okay, and is re-stoked for another while; 2) Cold smoke preserves rather than cooks; 3) Cold smoke imparts more delicate flavor; 4) Cold smoke is associated with fewer health concerns, namely polycyclic aromatic hydrocarbons, and; 4) Cold smoke allows for more diversity, as it is the choicest type of smoke for cheeses and vegetables, in addition to curing meats.

What is important to remember about cold smoking is that salt curing of meats is required before cold smoking can be preservative, and that cold smoked items may need to be cooked afterward, unless you are smoking cured meats long enough to induce a 30-50% weight loss. The same markers for shelf stability in fermented products apply to cold smoked products; that is, a pH lower than 5.2, and water activity lower than 0.82.

In any type of smoking, it is important to understand that the weather where you are living will affect the smoking conditions, as will the type of wood you are using. The flavors from smoking come from the components of the wood: hemicellulose, cellulose and lignin. Different wood species have different ratios of these components in their wood and their bark. Higher lignin lends to hotter fires, and hotter fires make these compounds burn more aggressively, which contributes to stronger flavors. Knowing this helps you understand why cold smoke imparts lighter flavor, as the smoke is cooler and more removed from the food; only the sweetest and most delicate volatile compounds remain when the smoke hits the food. Bark is higher in lignin than any other part of the tree, so many people knock it off of wood before smoking. Also, coniferous wood contains more lignin than hardwood species, so you will not find many people smoking with pine, cedar, cypress, or their brethren.

In general, artful smoking involves keeping temperatures *down*. Even in hot smoking, you are aiming for far lower temperatures than you have encountered in grilling. For best results, you want a smoldering fire, not an open flame. If you are a real geek, you can temp your firebox as well as your smoke chamber where the meat is. Optimum release of wood smoke's flavoring compounds has been recorded with fires right at 400°F.

The other consideration is humidity. Smoke adheres better, and Maillard browning reactions occur (in warm and hot smoking applications) more readily, when the food product is drier. This is chiefly why we hang cured meats and sausages to dry before smoking. Keep in mind, however, that condensation will build up in the smoke chamber as the meat loses moisture and the smoke condenses. It is a good idea to monitor the humidity in the smoke chamber of your smoker, just as you monitor humidity in your charcuterie cabinet. The optimum humidity in the smoke chamber should be 75–85%. You can combat a build-up of condensation by altering the roof design of your smoke chamber; by ensuring proper ventilation, both in the outlets you provide for the smoke; and in the ways you introduce airflow to the chamber.

Finally, the moisture in your wood relates directly to how it burns. The drier the wood, the more appropriate it is for cold smoking, between 15–20%. For hot smoking, fresh cut wood with moisture content of 40–60% is fine.

BUILDING YOUR OWN COLD SMOKER

With all of the above in mind, you can understand why building your own smoker might be a good idea. It will give you control over the system to help you achieve the type of smoke you desire. Most commercially available smokers are either electric or direct-heat type models. For ultimate cold smoking control, I have found that designing my own units has been a spectacular learning process, giving me a better understanding of working with wood and fire, as well as providing better results for my smoked meat projects.

The good news is that a smoker really only needs to keep a steady temperature, and hold smoke. These are the main requirements. Because of this, you can literally make a cold smoker from a cardboard box. All you need is a way to heat wood to low temperatures, pass the smoke from that wood to a separate chamber which holds the meat, and some ventilation or outlet for that smoke, once it comes in contact with the meat. If you search online you will find hundreds of designs, including smokers made of old kitchen cabinets, refrigerators, filing cabinets, etc. They are all good, as long as they meet the main criteria.

You'll need to come up with three main parts: a firebox, a pipe and a smoke chamber.

The Firebox

This is often the hardest part to construct. The firebox needs to be able to hold a fire (400°F+). Metal, ceramic, stone, brick, concrete, or other materials are the best bet. In addition to housing the heat, the firebox needs to have built-in ways for you to manage temperature. If you have any experience with fire, you know that it is alive — you kill it or help it thrive with oxygen and food. Built-in dampers are the way to manage the fire's strength and therefore its temperature. The more air you give a fire, and the more fuel via wood, the hotter it will burn. The less air, the slower and cooler the burn. Dampers can be as simple as lids that can be cocked to the side to allow airflow or closed to prevent it, or as complex as welded slides or swiveling covers placed strategically on the firebox. You'll need an opening for a pipe at or near the top of the firebox. As the smoke rises off of the fire, this will give it the easiest path to its eventual destination in the smoke chamber.

The Pipe

The pipe takes the smoke from the fire to the smoke chamber. It does not need to be insulated, as we are not concerned with whether the smoke cools. In fact, depending on the distance from the fire to the smoke chamber, some smoke cooling might be exactly what you want. So you can get away with cheaper options, such as stove pipe, dryer vent or metal scrap yard finds. In general, 4–6-inch diameter is best for getting a decent but conservative amount of smoke onto the food product. Remember, cold smoking is about light smoking, but you do not want to restrict the flow of smoke from the fire, as this would defeat the entire purpose.

To assist in smoke delivery, you need an incline in your pipe, to facilitate draft, or pull of the smoke through the system. A 5–10-degree angle is sufficient.

The Smoke Chamber

This is the cooler end of the equation, where the food is hung or placed on racks. Temperatures in the chamber should not exceed 80–100°F, which is why the smoke chamber can be made of cardboard, kitchen cabinets, pots, refrigerators, or other upcycled items. Remember that moisture is a consideration; so if you are using boxes, know that you may need to replace them now and again.

One of the main design requirements for the smoke chamber is that it be big enough to accommodate your meat projects. I find that height is the most important consideration there. If I have a strip of linked sausages, or large ham to smoke, I need at least 2–3 feet in order to hang it in a way that lets the smoke circle all around it. Similarly, you'll need hooks or rods at or near the top of the smoke chamber to support the weight of the products. A culatello, smoked for speck, can weigh 16 pounds, which is no job for flimsy hardware. Smoke hooks can be made with U-bolts or screw-hooks, or you can fashion up smokesticks using dowel rods or stainless steel rods. From the rods you can hang twine, bacon hangers or S-hooks.

Another design requirement is a smoke outlet. A hole somewhere near the top of the smoke chamber works, and can be covered with screen to prevent insects from entering the system. People also use stovepipe vents or louvers to achieve ventilation. Just be sure to monitor the set-up as you start using it. Clients often call me with problems related to humidity, and this is directly related to ventilation in the smoke chamber — most often, *not enough* of it. I like to think of smoke like I think of water. Plant roots grow great when the water can flow around them, but once it gets logged around the roots, you get rot. When smoke lingers and stales, you get bitterness and pungency. When it can flow from the low place of a smoldering fire up through the pipe, and then from the bottom to the top of the smoke chamber quite easily, you get delicate, sweet aroma, beautiful color, and fantastic flavor.

FINISHING SMOKED PRODUCTS

Most cold smoked meat products are either destined for further hanging and drying (as in nduja or speck) or are being cold smoked until they reach a shelf-stable water activity, indicated by a 40–50% weight loss. Either way, you'll want to pull the meat from the cold smoker and let it rest before storing it or returning it to the charcuterie chamber. Depending on smokehouse temperatures, you may want to cool the product with fans or a plunge in water once it has smoked, to prevent it shrinking away from its casing too drastically as it cools slowly. The water plunge is rather drastic, and usually only used when temperatures in the smoke chamber get over 150°F. Ideally, this will not happen in a cold smoker; if you are cold smoking meat successfully, you should be able to let the meat rest and cool naturally. If you need to speed the process, consider a box fan before an ice bath. Your aim is to progressively dehydrate the meat. Keeping conditions as dry as possible will aid you in this process.

Below are three smokers that I have designed, and continue to use. Each is quite suitable, depending on the nature of the food project.

▶ Terra cotta portable smoker

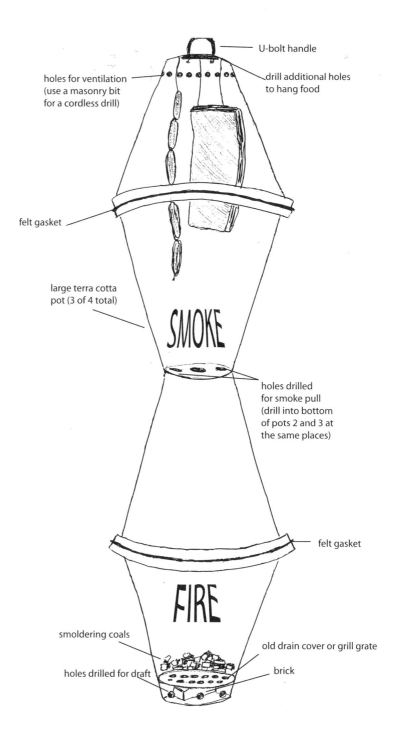

U-bolt handle

drill additional holes
to hang food

holes for ventilation
(use a masonry bit
for a cordless drill)

felt gasket

large terra cotta
pot (3 of 4 total)

SMOKE

holes drilled
for smoke pull
(drill into bottom
of pots 2 and 3 at
the same places)

felt gasket

FIRE

smoldering coals

old drain cover or grill grate

holes drilled for draft

brick

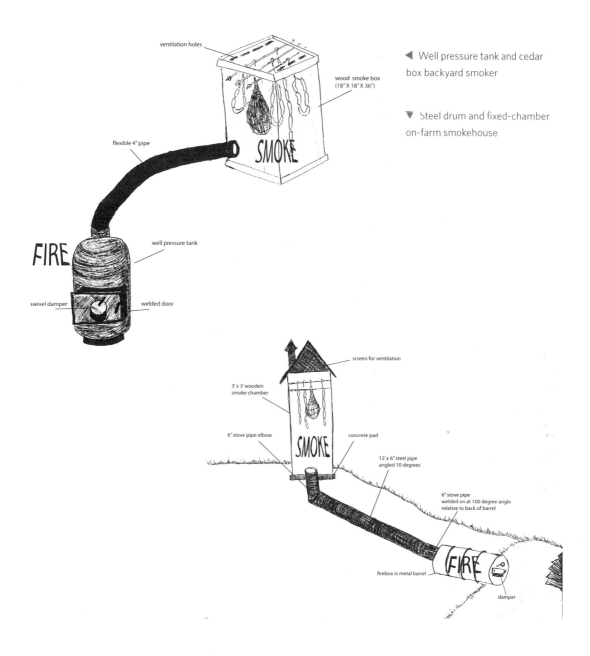

ventilation holes

wood smoke box
(18" X 18" X 36")

◀ Well pressure tank and cedar
box backyard smoker

▼ Steel drum and fixed-chamber
on-farm smokehouse

flexible 4" pipe

SMOKE

well pressure tank

FIRE

swivel damper   welded door

screen for ventilation

3' x 3' wooden
smoke chamber

6" stove pipe elbow   concrete pad

SMOKE

12' x 6" steel pipe
angled 10 degrees

6" stove pipe
welded on at 100 degree angle
relative to back of barrel

FIRE

firebox is metal barrel

damper

▲ Weston meat slicer

▲ So Apero salami slicer

SERVING AND STORING CHARCUTERIE

One of the most striking things about charcuterie is its powerful, complex flavor. As such, charcuterie is almost always served in very small portions. This is one of its chief triumphs, in my mind. We live in a society that over-values hugeness, and indeed, the more devoid of meaning and flavor our consumables have become, the bigger and bigger they have gotten, as if more of something is substitute for goodness in anything.

Currently, we find ourselves without widespread ethical meat production, slowly working toward mainstream adoption of ethical meat consumption, and lacking an ingrained competency in ethical meat preparation. I believe charcuterie, in light of the conditions here and now, can play a vital role in the revivification of a proper culinary mindset. If our understanding of portion size, our patience for process, and our palate's adoption of flavor must change, what better gateway do we have than charcuterie? It is possible that cured meat can be, or already is, more than just a fad. It may be old in its tradition and technique, but it is also new in its suggestion that this be a way to eat meat: tiny, delectable and time cured.

That being said, I find that charcuterie that isn't portioned properly can be pretty unsavory. Overbearing and salty might be better words for it. Doing justice to your time and creativity means investing in the proper tools for slicing, serving and storing. I have found that in this arena of food production, perhaps more so than others, you get what you pay for.

I use a Weston Pro 320 10-inch stainless steel meat slicer to slice pretty much everything, from salamis to coppa to smoked hams. I've tried a few different companies and this machine is by the far the best I've had on the home scale, though it is more expensive than other home slicers. I also use a Weston Pro 2300 Vacuum Sealer, which easily allows me to vacuum seal most of my projects for safe keeping. This method of storage removes all oxygen from the packaging, allowing you to keep shelf-stable products in a cool cabinet and smoked or cooked products (or sliced products) safely untainted in the fridge; it will also be your go-to for freezing cured meats, if you absolutely need to. I have also used So Apero products, crafted in France, for slicing, and in general really like them. They are not as adaptable for different-sized meat preparations, so you'll have to "buy up" when you're ready to slice bigger hams. Their cheaper models are smaller, and suitable for salamis, bresaola, and other smaller projects.

In general, store your whole or sliced, vacuum-sealed cured meats in a dark, cool place. Larger dried hams like prosciutto and culatello can be removed from the charcuterie cabinet, sliced to accommodate your needs, then wrapped in cheesecloth and returned to the charcuterie cabinet to age further.

Lastly, you can seal the surfaces of cured meat with fat. Of course! This is where it all began, after all. It is quite simple. Render lard by melting fat at low temperatures until you can't melt it anymore. Strain out the solids, then cool the liquid lard that remains. When it is whitened but still pliable, combine it with rice flour to produce a soft icing-like consistency. Black pepper doesn't hurt this mix, either. You can spread the fat mixture over the exposed surfaces of cold smoked or air cured items that you want to store for longer periods of time.

ADDITIONAL RECIPES

Things you'll make to put in your meat projects, and around them on the serving board.

HOMEMADE HORSERADISH

INGREDIENTS

½ cup grated
     horseradish root
¾ cup crème fraîche
1 Tbsp mustard
1 tsp white vinegar
Salt and pepper to taste

Method

1. Get some gloves on. Peel the horseradish root and grate it into the bowl of a food processor. Try not to breathe too deeply of the aroma; it can really knock you back. Add the rest of the ingredients to the food processor with the grated root and process to a creamy consistency. Store in the fridge, after you've portioned out what you need for Apple Horseradish Sausage (page 29).

HOMEMADE MISO SAUCE

INGREDIENTS

6 Tbsp light miso
¾ cup white wine
1 tsp sugar
1 Tbsp mirin
2 Tbsp rice vinegar

Method

You can put this on fish and soba noodles and in soup, in addition to using it in Miso & Pickled Ginger Sausage (page 30).

1. Pour the white wine, vinegar, sugar and mirin into a small bowl. With quick but gentle strokes, stir in the miso until it is dissolved. Store in a jar in the fridge until ready to use. This sauce is great on fish, too.

PICKLED GINGER

INGREDIENTS

1 cup fresh ginger, very thinly
     sliced or minced
⅓ cup white vinegar
⅔ cup water
1 tsp sugar

Method

1. Place the sliced or fine-diced ginger in a clean half-pint jar. Set aside. Combine the vinegar, water and sugar in a small saucepan and bring mixture just to a boil. Pour the hot brine over the diced ginger in the jar and cover with a lid. Cool completely to room temperature, then store in the fridge.

FERMENTED SWEET PEPPER

Method

1. Per 5 lb. of minced sweet pepper, add 3 Tbsp of sea salt. Mix well and pack into a jar. Leave to ferment at least 4 weeks, if not longer. In addition to using this in your pâté gratin (page 48), the ferment pairs well with root vegetables, winter squashes, mild cheeses and lamb.

INGREDIENTS

Assorted, colorful
    sweet peppers
Sea salt

FIG CHUTNEY

Method

1. Mix all ingredients and pack into a quart jar. Cover. Allow to ferment 2 days before refrigerating.

INGREDIENTS

4 C. figs, stemmed and
    quarteredlzl
½ t.· ground coriander
½ t. whole cloves
grated rind and juice of one
    orange
⅛ C. rapadura, or maple
    syrup
1–2 inches fresh ginger,
    peeled and grated on
    a zester or microplane
    grater
10–12 mint leaves, chopped
    fine
¼ C. whey
2 t. sea salt
½ C water

PICKLED CELERY LEAVES

INGREDIENTS

Leaves from celery heads,
   enough to fill a pint jar,
   chopped
Pinch of red pepper flake
Zest from ½ lemon, or ½
   confit lemon peel, diced
   and blanched
1 tsp fresh grated nutmeg
¾ cup white wine vinegar
1.5 cup water
2 tsp cane sugar (optional)

This is by far one of my favorite ideas I have ever had. I keep celery leaves out of my vegetable broth because they make it too pungent. I don't want to waste them, so I pickle them with confit lemon and nutmeg. The results are fantastic, and aside from using them in salami (page 104), I can put them in soups, stews, sausages, meat marinades, and even homemade Bloody Mary mix.

Method

1. Stuff the chopped celery leaves into the jar with the pepper flake, lemon zest or confit lemon, and nutmeg. Set aside. In a small saucepan, heat the water, vinegar and sugar just until it boils. Pour the boiling brine over the celery leaves and put a lid on the jar. Allow to cool to room temperature, then transfer to the fridge to cool completely.

FENNEL PICKLES

INGREDIENTS

Per 1–2 fennel bulbs,
   trimmed and
   thinly sliced:
½ cup non-chlorinated
   water
3 Tbsp cane sugar
2 garlic cloves, minced
1 tsp red pepper flake
1 tsp whole yellow
   mustard seed
2 Tbsp orange zest
1 tsp sea salt

I adore this fermented pickle in tomato soup, on grilled sandwiches, and as an accompaniment on the charcuterie board.

Method

1. Place all ingredients in a large bowl, and punch and squeeze everything with your hands until you've released the fennel's juices and melded all the ingredients well. Pack into an airlock jar and leave to ferment at room temperature at least two weeks. You can also pack into a mason jar, if you like, but you'll need to weigh the fennel mixture down so that it is underneath its liquid brine as it ferments. You can accomplish this with a smaller jar, washed and pushed down on top of the fennel mixture, then forced down with the lid of the fennel mixture's own jar.

CANDIED JALAPEÑO PEPPER

You'll want to double or triple this recipe, though.

Method

1. In a medium saucepan, stir together the vinegar and the sugar, and add the jalapeño slices. Bring to a low boil and simmer, until the jalapeño is tender but not mushy. Cut off the heat, and using a slotted spoon, remove the jalapeños from the syrup and packing them into the mason jar. Pour the hot syrup over the jalapeños, to cover, then put the lid on the jar and cool to room temperature. Then store in the fridge.

INGREDIENTS

Pint mason jar with lid

16 oz. jalapeño pepper, sliced thinly, with or without seeds (wear gloves!)

5 oz. white vinegar

2 oz. apple cider vinegar

2½ to 2⅔ cups cane sugar

PIMENTO CHEESE SPREAD

Not your Grandma's.

Method

1. Mix everything but the mayonnaise and cream cheese in a bowl. Add cream cheese and mayonnaise in small quantities, until you get the consistency you'd like. Chill the spread well. Taste, and season some more as your taste buds advise.

INGREDIENTS

2 cups shredded cheese. A mix is nice. Some sharp cheddar, some gouda, etc.

Some plain cream cheese

Some mayonnaise

A pinch of mustard seed

1 cup fermented sweet pepper (see above)

2 Tbsp candied jalapeño, diced (see above)

2–3 cloves of confit garlic (see Pork Shank Confit, page 76)

Salt to taste

Black pepper to taste

You cannot scream at the world
no matter what you know

from
behind your sunglasses,
your gorgeous
tattooed
blogroll.

it doesn't matter what you know

you have to feed the world

not a feast
just a bit of
sugar on a biscuit

if that's your thing
or
a drum beginning,

one
single silent stroke
of color.

Wear your story
on your skin, be it

a smell of burning
that echoes
a curse word,
a moment of pain.

Everything is food
that's alive,
requires work,

or if it comes with
a side of pickles

or burns the back of the throat.

Everything is a metaphor so
ruin some shirts,
loathe the sucking
of fingers
but record it
overtop the sweet
sounds of your laughter.

Everything is food
get your bib
get your spade

you cannot drive thru
this
is one way
with no window.

Everything is delicious
that reminds
us

and shows us our small
and
amazing
lives
going by
too fast.

RESOURCES

BOOKS

*The Ethical Meat Handbook: Complete Home Butchery, Charcuterie &
Cooking for the Conscious Omnivore* by Meredith Leigh, New Society
Publishers, 2015

Butchering Beef and Butchering Poultry, Rabbit, Lamb, Goat and Pork by
Adam Danforth, Storey Publishing, 2014

The Art of Charcuterie by John Kowalski, The Culinary Institute of
America, 2011

Charcuterie & French Pork Cookery by Jane Grigson, Penguin Books, 1967

The Art of Making Fermented Sausages by Stanley & Adam Marianski,
Book Magic, 2nd Edition, 2012

SUPPLIERS

Butcher and Packer (butcher-packer.com)

The Craft Butcher's Pantry (butcherspantry.com)

Weston Supply (westonsupply.com)

Sausage Maker (sausagemaker.com)

LEM (lemproducts.com)

GEM (gemcultures.com)

ACKNOWLEDGMENTS

THANKS TO MY colleagues, most especially Rocco Sinicrope and Dan Hettinger, who are both owed credit for smoker design. Thanks Ingrid, mama duck. Thanks to Jeremy Umansky. Thanks to my teachers and my students of butchery, curing and cooking (there are too many of you to name). Thanks to the farmers, every day, the earth, the leaves and seeds and beasts. Thanks to my family. Thanks Josh, I love you so big I can't believe it. Ela, Rose, Cash, Tucker: love, love, love, love.

ABOUT THE AUTHOR

OVER THE PAST fifteen years, Meredith Leigh has worked as a farmer, chef, teacher, nonprofit executive director, and writer, all in pursuit of sustainable food. She has developed a farmers cooperative, catalyzed nonprofit farm ventures, raised flowers, vegetables, and pastured meats, owned and managed a retail butcher shop, and more. Currently Meredith lives and teaches, handles sheep, cooks, and does outreach at Living Web Farms, a nonprofit educational and research farm in Mills River, NC. She is mother to two boys, many plants and numerous fermentation projects.

by Erin Adams

A NOTE ABOUT THE PUBLISHER

New Society Publishers is an activist, solutions-oriented publisher focused on publishing books for a world of change. Our books offer tips, tools, and insights from leading experts in sustainable building, homesteading, climate change, environment, conscientious commerce, renewable energy, and more — positive solutions for troubled times.

We're proud to hold to the highest environmental and social standards of any publisher in North America. This is why some of our books might cost a little more. We think it's worth it!

- We print all our books in North America, never overseas
- All our books are printed on 100% post-consumer recycled paper, processed chlorine free, with low-VOC vegetable-based inks (since 2002)
- Our corporate structure is an innovative employee shareholder agreement, so we're one-third employee-owned (since 2015)
- We're carbon-neutral (since 2006)
- We're certified as a B Corporation (since 2016)

At New Society Publishers, we care deeply about *what* we publish—but also about *how* we do business.

New Society Publishers	
ENVIRONMENTAL BENEFITS STATEMENT	
For every 5,000 books printed, New Society saves the following resources:[1]	
19	Trees
1,752	Pounds of Solid Waste
1,927	Gallons of Water
2,514	Kilowatt Hours of Electricity
3,184	Pounds of Greenhouse Gases
14	Pounds of HAPs, VOCs, and AOX Combined
5	Cubic Yards of Landfill Space

[1]Environmental benefits are calculated based on research done by the Environmental Defense Fund and other members of the Paper Task Force who study the environmental impacts of the paper industry.